AMERICA VERSUS THE TEN COMMANDMENTS

Exploring One Nation's Commitment to Biblical Morality

Michael K. Abel and Brent J. Schmidt

ISBN 978-1-64300-120-3 (Paperback)
ISBN 978-1-64300-121-0 (Hardcover)
ISBN 978-1-64300-122-7 (Digital)

Covenant Books, Inc.
11661 Hwy 707
Murrells Inlet, SC 29576
www.covenantbooks.com

To Patty, Craig, Kavyn, Bethany, Saydee, Brian, and Greysen who make it clear to me that there is moral truth in the world and it can be discovered if we look in the right place.

To Ross, my Hebrew teacher, who helped me treasure the Ten Commandments.

CONTENTS

ACKNOWLEDGMENTS

So many family members, friends, and colleagues provided encouragement and support throughout this process for which we are deeply grateful. Michael H. Abel, in particular, spent many hours reviewing and editing various drafts of the manuscript. His ability to edit with such speed and thoroughness was impressive. Avram R. Shannon and Samuel J. C. Smith, specialists in Hebrew literature, provided valuable commentary, feedback, and suggestions that were helpful in improving the manuscript at its earliest stages. Ross D. Baron also offered important insights into the Hebrew interpretations of the Ten Commandments that allowed for the identification of more effective measures than we would have used otherwise. Many sociologists, including Andrew E. Burger, Jeffrey R. Oliver, and Karin M. Abel examined the data analysis and provided helpful suggestions about how to present and organize it better. Many others reviewed early sections of the manuscript and helped us avoid being overly academic in our approach and writing style. We also appreciate the many researchers and organizations that spent time and resources collecting the data that made it possible to explore American commitment to the Ten Commandments and Maureen Kinley and the editors, typesetters, and cover designers who worked hard to help us turn our manuscript into a book. Whatever errors or oversights still remain are certainly our own.

PREFACE

Even before the courts issued mandates to remove the Ten Commandments from public spaces, the battle over what it means to be moral has long been waged. Traditionally, the dictates of the Ten Commandments, also known as the Decalogue, have been consistent with the moral leanings of the vast majority of Americans. More recently, however, increasingly loud voices have sought to not only regulate where the commandments (or other religious symbols) maybe displayed but also whether society should enforce compliance with or acknowledge the value of them at all. Indeed, some Americans seem to be moving away from traditional attitudes and behaviors while others seem to be holding on to longstanding views of right and wrong. It is from this context of moral conflict that the idea for this book emerged. In fact, its genesis is rooted in one simple question: "Do Americans keep the Ten Commandments?"

We assume we are not alone in wondering whether Americans are conducting their daily lives according to the traditional values of the Ten Commandments. Being as diverse as it is with so many faiths, traditions, cultures, and values, and being founded on Judeo-Christian principles, the United States of America has historically been considered by many to be a beacon of light in the darkness or a shining city on a hill. While some consider the establishment of *all* the standards set forth by the Ten Commandments to be essential for maintaining a harmonious, peaceful, and moral society, others are less convinced and are seeking to change certain long-held American values. Many argue that the moral culture of the United States is slipping away from its divinely established roots while others argue that the US society is simply embracing more liberties in accordance with the progressive and enlightened ideals of modern human rights.

No matter how one feels about the "culture wars," moral judgments about American mainstream culture are often casually made, and many statements regarding the Ten Commandments are, at best, educated guesses and, at worst, outright lies. Indeed, a survey done by Pew Research Center in 2010 found that a significant number of Americans cannot even correctly identify them. Respondents were given four statements and asked to indicate which of them was *not* one of the Ten Commandments. The statements included "Do not commit adultery," "Do not steal," "Keep the Sabbath day holy," and "Do unto others as you would have them do unto you." Only about half of Americans knew the last statement was not among the Ten Commandments.[1]

It seems clear that as a society, we have much to learn about the Decalogue, and we feel it is imperative that the Ten Commandments be understood on their own terms through time before judgments can be made about whether the people of the United States follow or do not follow them.

Only with correct understanding can ideals derived from the Ten Commandments be properly evaluated and analyzed in their individualistic context as found in law, culture, and tradition. It is therefore essential that we should begin by exploring the cultural milieu of each of the Ten Commandments in its ancient Near Eastern setting and then carefully trace its meaning through Bible times up into modernity. This book will provide the background to analyze the meaning of the Ten Commandments for modern, cosmopolitan civilizations, thus allowing us to provide a more thoughtful examination of them in comparison to mainstream American culture.

The reader might be surprised to learn that the purpose of this book is not to arrive at a conclusion about the answer to the question that motivated the book in the first place. Instead, we hope to provide information that will allow individuals to come to their own conclusions. Ultimately, the purpose of this book is to inform,

---

[1] Pew Research Center. 2010. U.S. Religious Knowledge Survey. Retrieved November 15, 2017 (Pew Research Center's Forum on Religion & Public Life, May 19–June 6, 2010).

not judge. Are Americans keeping the Ten Commandments? In the end, each reader must use the evidence provided to decide for himself or herself how well or how poorly the American society is doing when compared to the Western ideals of the Decalogue. Only then can one regard America as benevolent or corrupt and in turn embrace reform according to traditional mores or decide that the Ten Commandments should be replaced with alternative and progressive values. Hopefully, all readers, whether secular or religious, liberal or conservative, progressive or traditional, and peoples of all nationalities, colors, and creeds will find something in this book that will be challenging, stimulating, thought-provoking, humorous, enlightening, or even sobering.

After pondering upon something eye-catching in this work, we hope each reader will reflect on what universal principles and values are desirable in human societies. If one regards some of the Ten Commandments as outdated, quaint, or even reactionary, it would be necessary to replace them with other ideals or values in order that society might effectively function—ideally better than it does now. We hope the ideas and evidence provided in this work will inspire grander thinking about what it means to be a moral society and how we can tell if we have achieved it. We hope readers will ponder what it means to live a good, moral life and whether or not they are living one. These can be complicated questions, and proposed answers to them already fill more pages than one can read in a lifetime. Still we hope our work will prompt readers to either begin to think deeply about what is morally right and true and best for society and themselves or to consider issues of morality more completely than they have in the past.

Michael K. Abel and Brent J. Schmidt
January 2018

INTRODUCTION

What Is a Commandment?

The English word *commandment* is a translation of the frequently occurring Hebrew word *mitzvah*, meaning commandment or moral action. Its first biblical occurrence is in Genesis 26:5 (KJV) when God states that "Abraham obeyed my voice, and kept my charge, my commandments, my statutes and my laws." In the Abrahamic faiths (Judaism, Christianity, and Islam), commandments derive from God's perceived divine will. In this way, commandments constitute divinely sanctioned rules of conduct. Judaism traditionally divides commandments into two major groups, positive and negative ones. Generally positive commandments were considered obligations while negative commandments often became prohibitions. During the Hellenistic or "Greek-like" age (beginning in 323 BCE), when Greek became the international language of the Mediterranean and Middle East, the Greek noun *entolē*, meaning *commandment* or *rule*, was sometimes used to render *mitzvah*. Funeral inscriptions of Jewish tombs of this period contain the Greek epithet *phil-entolos*, literally meaning "lover of the commandments." This Greek noun (*entolē*) was used throughout the Greek New Testament to refer to Jesus's precepts, teachings, commandments, or rules.

Interestingly, the Hebrew term *dabar*, which means *word*, is used in Exodus 20 where the Ten Commandments are first introduced in the Old Testament. Accordingly, the term *Decalogue* (Greek: *deka-logoi*), or the "Ten Words" in ancient Greek, literally expresses the Hebrew *dabar* (meaning *word* or *thing*) of God. The "Ten Words," derived from Exodus 34:28, Deuteronomy

1

4:13, and Deuteronomy 10, simply describe the ten obligations and prohibitions given to Moses by God as part of the Mosaic Law. Josephus (AD 37–100), a Greek-speaking Jew of New Testament times, referred to each particular commandment of the Decalogue as an individual *logos* (meaning *commandment* here) in his famous work *Antiquities of the Jews* (3.91). In ancient Greek, *logos* can be translated in dozens of ways because it was associated with many pagan subjects including politics, warfare, philosophy, mythology, and religion. Philo (25 BCE–50 CE), a Greek-speaking Jew who lived in Roman times, considered a *logos* in this context as an oracle.[2] Today it is often rendered by Bible translators as *word, commandment, speech, rationality,* or even *reason. Logos* simultaneously held all these meanings and many more in deeply pious ancient Mediterranean societies where almost everything was inherently religious. In ancient Greek, there was not even a specific word for religion because it transcended everything.

From early biblical times, up until at least the French Revolution, *command* or *word* always implied obligations, rules, and conduct derived from divine law. Kings, priests, judges, emperors, generals, and other leaders of the ancient Mediterranean world were believed to rule by divine right. Commandments from these rulers at times came in the form of orders, demands, obligations, duties, and rules and were sealed by perceived divine authority that persisted up through the middle ages until the secular age which began during the Enlightenment (eighteenth century). Only in recent times has western society been divided up into religious and secular spheres often known today as church and state.

---

[2] Philo *Decalogue* 32; (All quotations from the *Decalogue* are from Philo *On the Decalogue, On the Special Laws, On the Virtues* in the Loeb Classical Library, 320, ed. E. H. Warmington, trans. F. H. Colson (Cambridge: Harvard University, 1998) https://ryanfb.github.io/loebolus-data/L320.pdf

The Origin of the Ten Commandments

There are two common explanations of the origin of the Ten Commandments or the Decalogue. One is scriptural, traditional, and orthodox, while the other would be considered secular. This traditional explanation is found in Exodus 34:28 (NIV): "Moses was there with the LORD forty days and forty nights without eating bread or drinking water. And he wrote on the tablets the words of the covenant—Ten Commandments." There were two tablets, one with the commandments and the other to have an extra and exact legal copy as part of making a covenant, and they were written on both sides (Exodus 32:15), which has been well attested in the ancient Near East.[3] Although Moses was Jehovah's servant who wrote them down, tradition states that God himself is their author. These

---

[3] Nahum M. Sarna *The JPS Torah Commentary: Exodus* (New York: JPS, 1991), 108, noted: Several biblical texts testify to the inscribing of the Decalogue on two stone tablets. The practice of recording covenants on tablets was well rooted in the biblical world, as was also the custom, mentioned in Exodus 25:16, of depositing the document in the sanctuary. A treaty between the Hittite King Shuppiluliumas (ca. 1375–1335 BCE) and King Mattiwaza of Mittani in Upper Mesopotamia noted that each of the contracting parties deposited a copy in his respective temple before the shrine of the deity. Similarly, when Ramses II of Egypt and the Hittite King Hattusilis concluded a treaty around the year 1269 BCE, the clauses were inscribed on a tablet of silver, which was placed "at the feet of the god." In Rome, too, treaties (Latin *foedera*) were written on tablets—bronze—and stored in the Capitol. Michael Coogan *The Ten Commandments: A Short History of an Ancient Text* (New Haven: Yale University Press, 2014), 18. Coogan wrote, In most legal systems, each party to a contract gets a copy of what they have agreed to. This is also true of ancient suzerainty treaties: duplicates of the treaty were deposited in the temple of the chief deities of both suzerain and vassal, because the gods, as witnesses, were the ultimate enforcers of the treaty. The text of the Decalogue was written on two tablets because each party—in this case, God and the Israelites—was to get a copy of it. Moreover, the tablets of the Decalogue were deposited in the "ark of the covenant," originally, as we will see, a kind of sacred safe-deposit box kept in the innermost sanctum of an Israelite shrine. Some treaties also specify that they are to be read aloud publicly at regular intervals. So too, according to Deuteronomy, the divinely given law was to be read "every seven years . . . at the festival of Booths . . . before all Israel . . . men, women, and children" (Deut. 31:10–12).

Ten Commandments and other laws and ordinances were associated with Moses's interactions with God before receiving what eventually became known as the Mosaic Law in Judaism. The Decalogue has often been viewed as the essence of the Torah.[4]

Christians traditionally believe that Jesus indirectly endorsed and then transcended the Ten Commandments. Jesus emphasized loving God (Deuteronomy 6:4–6) and loving one's neighbor (Leviticus 19:18) from the Mosaic Law when he taught that there were but two commandments: One should love God and his neighbor because "on these two commandments hang all the law and the prophets" (Matthew 22:35–40). These two commandments promoted by Jesus were dependent on the law and prophets as taught in other sections of the Mosaic Law. In addition, when replying the young man asked, "What must I do to inherit eternal life?" Jesus replied, "You know the commandments, do not murder, do not commit adultery, do not steal, do not bear false witness, do not defraud, honor your father and mother" (Mark 10:19). In other words, Jesus quoted from the covenantal center of the Old Testament, the Ten Commandments, and teaches that proper performance of these commandments will result in eternal life. Jesus asserts that it is necessary to follow these commandments to attain eternal life.[5] Jesus also taught his disciples in the Sermon on the Mount, "Think not that I am come to destroy the law, or the prophets" (Matthew 5:17 KJV).

Both the Jews' and Christians' adherence to the Ten Commandments has led to remarkably similar values and law in the West—sometimes known as the Judeo-Christian tradition. In many ways though, some might argue that western culture is now drifting

---

[4] Mark F. Rooker *The Ten Commandments: Ethics for the 21ˢᵗ Century* (Nashville: B&H, 2010), 9, noted: The Ten Commandments have been viewed within Judaism as the essence of the Torah. Many have noted that all 613 laws of the Torah correspond to the 613 letters of the Ten Commandments in Exod. 20, hence the Decalogue appears to represent the embodiment of all laws and statutes of the Pentateuch. Since the first century BC, the Ten Commandments have been regarded as a summary of biblical law or as headings for all its categories.

[5] Matthew Bates *Salvation by Allegiance Alone* (Grand Rapids: Baker, 2017), 10.

away from these Judeo-Christian moorings as it has been influenced by modern ideologies including secular humanism, materialism, atheism, existentialism, and post-modernism.

One secular theory about the origin of the Ten Commandments postulates that they were man-made by later teachers and priests who examined written records and then created rules to guide the community.[6] The Ten Commandments received by Moses also resemble the covenant traditions of neighboring peoples, including Hittite state treaties.[7] Traditionalists might point out though that this does not necessary imply that the Ten Commandments were made up wholesale by later Israelites. It could just reflect the fact "that the Lord patterned His covenant relationship with Israel after the prevailing international political treaty form" which his people could then understand.[8]

---

[6] Calum M. Carmichael *The Ten Commandments* (Oxford: The Ninth Sacks Lecture, 1983), 27, noted: "If a guess were to be hazarded about the original setting in life of the Decalogue it would be that of teacher and pupils examining written records for the purpose of setting down rules, most of or all of which would already be known to them in some form or another. The indication is that Deuteronomic wisdom circles are responsible for their compilation. Of them we do know that the recipients of instruction could read and write (Deut. 6:9, 11:20). The ten 'words' were written, we are to believe, upon two tables of stone so that Moses might use them for instructional purposes (Ex. 24:12, Deut. 4:10). Two different experiences, it has been argued, went into their construction. The model in mind may well be two different school exercises whereby the teacher examined one body of material about the incident of the golden calf and another about the origin of mankind."

[7] Dan Lioy *The Decalogue in the Sermon on the Mount* Studies in Biblical Literature 66 (New York: Peter Lang, 2004), 46.

[8] Dan Lioy *The Decalogue in the Sermon on the Mount* Studies in Biblical Literature 66 (New York: Peter Lang, 2004), 46; Michael Coogan *The Ten Commandments: A Short History of An Ancient Text* (New Haven: Yale University Press, 2014), 14. Coogan noted that "when one was superior to another, the treaty is called a "suzerainty treaty," and the parties—the suzerain and his vassal, to use medieval terminology—often referred to each other as father and son, or master and servant (see, for example, 2 Kings 16:7). When the biblical writers used the term "covenant" to characterize the relationship between God and Israel, they had these legal analogues in mind: God was Israel's husband, owner, and ruler. The prophets Hosea, Jeremiah, and Ezekiel especially develop the marital metaphor;

While there has been much scholarly speculation about the origin of the Ten Commandments, the strongest believers are confident in their divine origin while secularists are certain they are a purely human construction. Yet others may conclude it must be a combination of both. Traditionalists tend to use the Decalogue as given in Exodus 20 while secular commentators have noted that there are three different versions of it and there are many differences among them. Michael Coogan in his recent secular work *The Ten Commandments* has an entire chapter dedicated to this subject titled "Which Version of the Ten Commandments," which details differences between Exodus 20, 34, and Deuteronomy 5.[9] Coogan argues that because there are different versions of the Decalogue, it becomes problematic when deciding as a multicultural American society about which version should be displayed in governmental spaces. Whatever one decides about its origins or basic unity or disunity, certainly the Decalogue is viewed in the Judeo-Christian tradition as a covenantal law which God gave to his people after they had been delivered from bondage in Egypt. Some considered it a burden to have the Decalogue while others believed it was a gift and a privilege that, when observed, continually renewed this special covenant relationship between Israel and God. Because of this covenantal relationship, Israel was expected to demonstrate gratitude to God by keeping all of the Ten Commandments.[10] The Decalogue occupied a central place in the history of ancient Israel and eventually its norms became the basis of the three great Abrahamic religions: Judaism, Christianity, and Islam.

---

some legal texts speak of God as Israel's owner; and the Psalms and other texts often refer to God as king. The last metaphor is especially pertinent."

[9] Michael Coogan *The Ten Commandments: A Short History of an Ancient Text* (New Haven: Yale University Press, 2014), 25-34.

[10] J. J. Stamm with M. E. Andrew *The Ten Commandments in Recent Research Studies in Biblical Theology* Second Series 2 (Naperville: Alec R. Allenson, Inc., 1967), 113–114.

The Ten Commandments as God's Eternal Law

The Ten Commandments were associated with God's law for all times. A religious system like Judaism has its most direct influence in life through social norms. Certainly, commandments play a role in religious life, which cannot be underestimated because, although often abstract, they provide orientation in life.[11] Moreover God's commandments represented his unfathomable wisdom: "Do you listen in on God's council? Do you have a monopoly on wisdom?" (Job 15:8). In Genesis, Joseph of Egypt was later perceived to have wisely kept the Ten Commandments before they were given as a precursor to a religious system. Figures of the Hebrew Bible are considered notable because keeping the commandments was their outstanding virtue or, conversely, are condemned because they did not keep these dictates. The Joseph narrative demonstrates the wise choices that Joseph made, which can be learned from following the principles of the Ten Commandments.[12]

In contrast, King David, who begins in the Biblical narrative as a hero, subsequently broke at least the sixth, seventh, eighth, and tenth commandments (arguably even all of them) in 2 Samuel 11 when he committed adultery, killed Uriah, and finally married Uriah's wife, Bathsheba. Although it did not seem to apply to the king, the penalty in the Hebrew Bible for breaking most of the Ten Commandments, except for coveting and certain forms of stealing, was death. However, it must be noted that the Decalogue does not specifically concern itself with the penalties for breaking commandments.[13]

---

[11] Gerd Thiessen *A Theory of Primitive Christian Religion* trans. John Bowden (London: SCM Press, 1999), 12.

[12] Ginzberg vol. 2 p. 183; Alan M. Dershowitz *The Genesis of Justice: Ten Stories of Biblical Injustice that Led to the Ten Commandments and Modern Law* (New York: Warner Books, 2000), 251–252.

[13] Nahum M. Sarna *The JPS Torah Commentary: Exodus* (New York: JPS, 1991), 115, for a discussion of the ideal of the Decalogue. For the prescribed punishment of the draconian punishment of death, see Bruce J. Malina and Richard L. Rohrbaugh Social-Science Commentary on the Synoptic Gospels 2nd Edition (Minneapolis: Fortress Press, 2003), 418–419. Malina summarizes the specific verses wherein death is prescribed as a punishment for vio-

In New Testament times, Israelites were strictly forbidden to recite the Ten Commandments verbatim because of their perceived sanctity. Josephus, a Jewish general of the first-century CE, reported (about 90 CE) that in his time, just as it was forbidden to utter the Tetragrammaton, YHWH, the most sacred name of the God of Israel, so too it was forbidden to utter the "Ten Words" given on Sinai to Israel. Nevertheless, Josephus indicates their "power" (*Antiquities of the Jews* 3.90). After all, these very words, "the Ten Commandments which God himself gave to his people without employing the agency of any prophet or interpreter were the direct words of the God of Israel himself, hence full of power."[14] Rabbinic tradition reports that among the texts recited daily in the Temple in Jerusalem were the Decalogue and three other passages from the Torah.[15] Jesus also built his new covenant upon the Ten Commandments when he taught principles that would enable his disciples to avoid even getting close to transgressing them by his teachings in the Sermon on the Mount. Jesus specifically proclaimed:

> Do not think that I have come to abolish
> the law or the prophets; I have come not to abol-

---

lations of the Decalogue: *Idolatry*: Those serving and worshiping other gods (Deuteronomy 17:7), as well as false prophets (Deuteronomy 13:5), are to be put to death. *Blasphemy*: Blasphemers of the name of the YHWH shall be put to death (Leviticus 24:16). *Sabbath Observance*: Infractions of the Sabbath require the death penalty for the offender (Exodus 31:14–15; 35:2; Numbers 15:35). *Parents*: The death penalty is required of anyone who strikes father or mother, or who curses father or mother (Exodus 21:15, 17; Leviticus 20:9); this is also the fate of a recalcitrant son disobedient to parents (Deuteronomy 21:21). *Adultery*: The death penalty is commanded for adulterer and adulteress (Deuteronomy 22:22), consenting betrothed woman and another man (Deuteronomy 22:24), rapist of unconsenting betrothed woman (Deut. 22:25), a wife without tokens of virginity (Deut. 22:21). *Murder*: "Whoever strikes a man so that he dies shall be put to death" (Exodus 21:12; also Numbers 35:16-21): murders must be put to death . . . *Kidnappers* must be put to death (Exodus 21:16; Deuteronomy 24:7). *False witnesses* are to be put to death (Deuteronomy 19:19).

14 Philo, *Special Laws* 3.2.7.

15 Mishnah Tamid 5.1; Berakot 11b; Michael Coogan *The Ten Commandments: A Short History of An Ancient Text* (New Haven: Yale University Press, 2014), 95.

ish but to fulfill. For truly I tell you, until heaven and earth pass away, not one letter, not one stroke of a letter, will pass from the law until all is accomplished. Therefore, whoever breaks one of the least of these commandments, and teaches others to do the same, will be called least in the kingdom of heaven; but whoever does them and teaches them will be called great in the kingdom of heaven. (Matthew 5:17–19 NRSV)

Parts of Jesus's Sermon on the Mount are founded upon principles of the Ten Commandments, although they are not quoted verbatim. Most Christians believe Jesus's commandments fulfilled and even transcended the Decalogue and thus created a New Covenant with his disciples. The apostle Paul later listed norms in this New Covenant.

Paul utilized the Decalogue to teach the good news of Christianity. He occasionally alluded to the Gentiles' "unnatural" sexual behavior contrary to Israel's covenant, and listed other "typical non-Israelite wickedness that likewise dishonors God, presenting an alternate listing of the Ten Commandments as follows: They were filled with all manner of wickedness: (1) evil, covetousness, (2) malice, envy, (3) murder, strife, (4) deceit, malignity, (5) gossips, slanders, (6) haters of God, (7) insolent, haughty, (8) boastful inventors of evil, disobedient to parents, (9) foolish, faithless, (10) heartless, ruthless (Rom. 1:29–32). Near the end of this letter to the Romans, Paul continued to cite the Decalogue with approval: "Do not owe anyone anything, except to love each other, for whoever loves his neighbor has fulfilled the law. For "Do not commit adultery; do not murder; do not steal; do not desire" and every other commandment that exists, is summed up in this saying: "Love your neighbor as yourself." Love does not do wrong to a neighbor; therefore love is the fulfillment of law"[16] (Romans 13:8–10). We find even more

---

[16] Michael Coogan *The Ten Commandments: A Short History of An Ancient Text* (New Haven: Yale University Press, 2014), 103

lists quoting principles from the Decalogue in 1 Corinthians 6:9–11 and 1 Timothy 1:9–11."[17] Other Christian writers also promoted ideals of the Ten Commandments because they believed that they were ordained by God and angels in Galatians 3:19, Acts 7:53, and Hebrews 2:2 that were later echoed in the writings of other Christian fathers.[18]

Philo, an educated Platonist Jew living in New Testament times, considered the Decalogue the cornerstone of the Mosaic Law. Concerning the overall focus of the Decalogue, he regarded the Ten Commandments as summary principles governing the entire Mosaic legislation in part because the number *decad* or ten embraces Nature as seen both with and without extension in space.[19] He furthermore divided these commandments into two groups of five on each of the two plates. Philo believed that the superior first group was concerned with service toward God while the second group was specifically concerned with prohibitions. Moreover, Philo asserted that only those who adhered to both of the two sections were completely virtuous—becoming simultaneously lovers of God and lovers of mankind.[20]

Of all the passages in the Old Testament, the Decalogue in particular is presumably the most promoted and best known to western civilization. For example, it has been extensively used by the Catholic faith for millennia. The Manichees, a group that was deemed heretical by the Catholic church in late Roman times, imposed on their ordinary members their own version of the Ten Commandments, which included "prohibitions of idolatry and witchcraft, covetousness, killing and adultery, lying, effeminacy, and neglect of their religious duty. They were required to confess to God and to the Elect and

---

[17] Bruce J. Malina and Richard L. Rohrbaugh *Social-Science Commentary on the Synoptic Gospels* 2nd Edition (Minneapolis: Fortress Press, 2003), 148.

18 . Solomon Goldman *The Ten Commandments* (Chicago: University of Chicago Press, 1956), 27:

[19] Philo *Decalogue* 24; Pythagorean and Platonic teachings about numbers emphasized that special numbers such as ten represented notions of harmony and other mystical and philosophical truths that were originally associated with mathematics.

[20] Dan Lioy, *The Decalogue in the Sermon on the Mount* Studies in Biblical Literature 66 (New York: Peter Lang, 2004), 37; Philo *Decalogue*, 50–51.

to observe certain fasts for fifty days in the year."[21] As a result of their combating divergent ideas about God, orthodox Christianity linked creeds, the Lord's Prayer, and the Ten Commandments in a catechism as the three most essential components of belief throughout the middle ages.[22] In the early fourteenth century, Louis of Bavaria was noted to have said the "Ave Maria" prayer so many times that it became a substitute for the Ten Commandments.[23]

During the Reformation, the Decalogue was used as a standard of Christian literacy. The famous reformer, Martin Luther (1483–1546), incorporated the Ten Commandments into his *Kleiner Katechismus* or instruction classes for converts.[24] For Luther, no one would ever be able to satisfy the demands of the Ten Commandments even though all Christians were expected to know them.[25] He believed Christians should fulfill the law not in order to be saved but because they are saved.[26] A church survey conducted in Gloucestershire, England, in 1551 by Bishop Hooper discovered that of 311 clerics, nine (3%) did not know how many commandments God gave to Moses on Sinai, 33 (11%) did not know where to find them in the Bible, and 168 (54%) could not repeat them by memory. In 1560, the London diocese prohibited 22 out of 56 clerics (39%) from practicing due to their ignorance.[27] Today the Ten Commandments have a special

---

[21] Gerald Bonner, *St. Augustine of Hippo: Life and Controversies* (Norwich: Canterbury Press, 1986), 172.

[22] *Creeds and Confessions of Faith in the Christian Tradition Volume: Early, Eastern, & Medieval* edited by Jaroslav Pelian & Valerie Hotchkiss (New Haven: Yale University Press, 2003), 20.

[23] William Ragsdale Cannon, *History of Christianity in the Middle Ages* (Nashville: Abingdon, 1960), 301–302.

[24] Eduard Nielsen, *The Ten Commandments in New Perspective* (London: SCM Press, 1968), 1.

[25] David M. Whitford, *A Reformation Life: The European Reformation through the Eyes of Philipp of Hesse* (Santa Barbara: Praeger, 2015), 50–51.

[26] David M. Whitford, *A Reformation Life: The European Reformation through the Eyes of Philipp of Hesse* (Santa Barbara: Praeger, 2015), 50–51.

[27] David Daniell, William Tyndale, A Biography (New Haven: Yale University Press, 1994), 78 and also found in S. Michael Wilcox Fire in the Bones: William Tyndale Martyr (Salt Lake City: Deseret, 2014)

significance to Jews and to Christians of many traditions, including both Catholic and Protestant.

Numbering the Ten Commandments

Numbering the Ten Commandments has varied somewhat among religious traditions over the last two millennia. The Roman Catholic and Lutheran churches have adopted a division made by Augustine in late Roman times, which has continued until the modern period. They treat verse 2 of Exodus 20 as a preamble and differ from the Jewish sources in counting verses 3–6 as the first, while dividing instruction about one's neighbor, into the ninth and tenth commandment. We will follow this traditional numbering throughout this work.

The Plan of the Book

As might be expected, this book comprises ten core chapters—one for each commandment. Every chapter consists of two main parts. The first is an exploration of the probable meaning of the commandment in its historical context. Each discussion is designed to promote deeper understanding of the intent of the commandment as it likely would have been understood in its original context and as later interpreted throughout ancient Biblical times, sometimes up until modern times. These discussions also provide the basis of how the commandments are interpreted for purposes of measurement and data analysis in our modern context.

In the second part of each chapter, various datasets and data sources are described and analyzed in an effort to paint a picture of American compliance with and commitment to the Ten Commandments. While we have done our best to find direct measures of obedience to the commandments, we have also included measures of people's beliefs and attitudes about keeping them and general issues surrounding them. Our analysis is meant to be descriptive and in no way purports to be an attempt to convince the reader of any particular position or conclusion about what it means for America to be committed to the Decalogue. We know it is no secret that some Americans strive to keep the Ten Commandments while others view compliance to at least some of them as unimportant. Our goal is to avoid providing our own biased commentary about how well America is adhering to biblical morality. To the best of our knowledge and abilities, the data is presented fairly and stands as its own conclusion. Additionally, we will not discuss whether or not Americans should support the way of life promoted by the Decalogue, only data that reflects the extent to which they do. In essence, we have simply tried to compile in one place information that reveals something about the extent to which Americans keep, and what they think and believe about keeping, the Ten Commandments.

Ultimately, we recognize that readers will not always agree with our chosen measures and that is understandable. In some cases, even we wish we had better data and other kinds of information to present to the reader. Unfortunately, for this project, we have been at the mercy of data that already exists. We hope future data collection endeavors do more to directly measure compliance with some of the Ten Commandments. Whether that happens or not, we have tried to align our measurements, as much as possible, with common understandings and interpretations of the Decalogue. We welcome any feedback about data sources that might include better measures than those presented here. Finally, we hope all, whether enthusiastic or not about our choices, will find the facts interesting to think about in the context of the topic.

While we trust that the analysis presented in this book accurately represents what Americans really say they think and do, we do not make any claims about how frequently people are telling the truth. All social scientists know there is a powerful pull in humans to respond to questions in ways that are socially desirable, sometimes at the expense of being truthful. While the reader must be aware of this phenomenon, he or she should also know that whenever possible, researchers go to great lengths, like keeping identities anonymous and carefully wording survey questions, to minimize the pressure respondents feel to say what they think others want to hear. Still, if you find yourself feeling skeptical about the percentage of Americans who say they would never cheat in a game of cards with people they do not know well, not even for a million dollars (see Chapter 9), please know you are not alone. Even so, while it is sometimes reasonable to be skeptical about the size of the numbers when social pressures are in play, we can say with confidence that findings related to the direction of trends over time and how groups generally compare to each other are typically accurate despite this.

In most chapters, adherence will be considered across age cohorts, with particular focus on comparing the youngest age group (eighteen- to twenty-nine-year-olds) to the oldest (sixty-year-olds and older). It seems relevant to the question of how we are doing in relation to the Ten Commandments to consider whether or not the morals and values presented therein are being passed to and accepted by younger generations. In most cases, these generational effects are quite striking. In order to prevent information overload, we have opted to keep our analysis simple. Our intent is not to test a hypothesis or to prove one group or cohort is better or worse off than another. Instead our goal is to give the reader very interesting and pertinent data to think about. While statistical conclusions are revealed, their ultimate meaning and relevance, including a final verdict on whether or not Americans are doing a good job keeping the Ten Commandments, will be left up to the reader.

Finally, it should be noted that there can be considerable overlap when it comes to matching modern attitudes and behaviors to specific commandments. For the sake of organization and to avoid repetition, we will resist the temptation to present the same data in multiple chapters, though a particular fact might reveal something about multiple commandments. Readers should not hesitate to make these connections. It would be entirely reasonable, for example, to consider how the prevalence of theft might relate to the commandment to avoid coveting, or link measures of coveting to how people prioritize God in their lives. Many such connections can be identified and making them is strongly encouraged.

COMMANDMENT 1

"Thou shalt have no other gods before me"

Although the first commandment was traditionally revealed to Moses on Mount Sinai, Abraham, the father of many nations including the faith traditions of Judaism, Christianity, and Islam, demonstrated throughout his difficult life why mankind should worship one God. Abraham's worship of God has been interpreted in many ways. Jews and Muslims generally regard the first commandment as a testimony of faith while some Christians may consider the Ten Commandments as a schoolmaster to proper and basic moral living. However, ancient legend surrounding the persona of Abraham instructed its hearers to ignore other gods because of their perceived inability to act for themselves. According to one midrash (an ancient commentary), Abraham's father, Terach (Terah), was a maker of idols. One day, Abraham "took a hatchet in his hand, and broke all his father's gods," except for the biggest one. When his father saw the smashed idols, he became angry, but Abraham shrewdly blamed their destruction on the largest of the idols in whose hand he had planted a hatchet. Terach became accusatory and in order to prove that the large idol had been framed, Terach argued: "Is there spirit, soul, or power in these Gods . . . ? Are they not wood and stone? Have I not myself made them?" Abraham retorted: "How, then canst thou serve these idols in whom there is no power to do anything?" Terach then took the hatchet from the hand of the large idol and smashed it, thus demonstrating his rejection of false gods, graven images, and idol worship.[28]Ancient listeners may have learned much from this anecdote about the religious necessity to reject materialism, to initiate self-help, and to accept appropriate kinds of religious violence. Modern readers also learn much about how to serve only one God as articulated after Abraham through the first commandment.

Before the notion of separation of church and state, nationalism, or even an accepted definition of religion, religious values permeated all aspects of life. Most ancient peoples worshiped the particular gods of their land. The commandment given to Moses, "to have no other God's before me" (Exodus 20:3) essentially barred obedience to any gods beside Yahweh forever.[29] Yahweh desired to have a special relationship with Israel in order to build a covenant community, but they could not have any other gods.[30] Despite the commandment to the contrary, Israelites often supported the worship of local deities. Several generations after this commandment had been given, David complained to Saul that he (David) had been unjustly driven out of his own land and encouraged to abandon the worship of Yahweh in order to worship of the gods of the land in which he was in exile. (1 Samuel 26:19).[31] In these early biblical times, an atheist was a fool (Psalm 14:1 and 53:1), misguided, or silly because he was out of step with his surroundings.[32]After they entered the land of Canaan, the Israelites were influenced by Canaanite religion and intermittently worshipped gods and goddesses such as Baal, Asherah, and Ashtoreth. The worship of Baal appears to have been widespread in the time of Judges (Judges 2:11; 3:7; 6:25, 29–30) and in the time of Samuel (1 Samuel 7:3–4) and after Solomon (1 Kings 11:5–7)

---

[28] Alan M. Dershowitz. *The Genesis of Justice: Ten Stories of Biblical Injustice that Led to the Ten Commandments and Modern Law* (New York: Warner Books, 2000), 247–249; Midrash Rabbah vol. 1, p. 214–215, 310. Louis Ginzberg. *The Legends of the Jews* (Baltimore: John Hopkins University Press, 1998), 214.

[29] H. C. Propp. *Exodus 19–40 The Anchor Bible* (New York: Doubleday, 2006), 167.

[30] John I. Durham. *Exodus Word Biblical Commentary* (Waco: Word, 1987), 285.

[31] R. H. Charles. *The Decalogue* (Eugene, OR: Wif and Stock, 2004), 4.

[32] Walter Harrelson. *The Ten Commandments and Human Rights* (Philadelphia: Fortress, 1980), 59.

and later under Ahab (1 Kings 16:31–32).[33] Later Israelite prophets and leaders pleaded, warned, and begged the children of Israel to worship Yahweh during cultural declines, war, famine, and exile, but often to no avail. Other gods were more appealing, either because they required little devotion—except for their perceived need to be appeased through ritual prostitution, sensuous festivals, and animal and occasionally human sacrifice, followed by cooked meat for the worshippers of the ritual animal offering.[34]

Neighboring ancient storytellers and thinkers in the Mediterranean skillfully described and promoted worship practices and beliefs about the gods or God throughout the known world. Herodotus, the Greek father of history, characterized these beliefs about the gods as relative and even derived from custom.[35] Another Greek thinker, Xenophanes of Colophon, also argued for one abstract, unknowable, and unapproachable God.[36] These Greek notions of an abstract God in time became extremely influential to others in the Mediterranean in later Hellenistic or Greek-like centuries before and during New Testament times. From comments in Hecataeus of Abdera and Strabo, Gentiles praised the Judeans' "phil-

---

[33] Mark F. Rooker. *The Ten Commandments: Ethics for the 21ˢᵗ Century* (Nashville: B&H, 2010), 28.

34 . Michael Coogan. *The Ten Commandments: A Short History of An Ancient Text* (New Haven: Yale University Press, 2014), 30. While Moses is communing with God, with the complicity of Moses's brother Aaron, the Israelites "made a golden calf and engaged in a ritual that the narrators hint included sexual orgy: "Early the next morning they offered burnt offerings and brought sacrifices of well-being. And the people sat down to eat and drink, and got up to play" (Exodus 32:6). The last word here can have sexual innuendo, as when King Abimelech observes Isaac "playing with" Rebekah, whom the patriarch had claimed was his sister, and the king exclaimed: "So she is your wife!" (Genesis 26:8–9)."

R. H. Charles *The Decalogue* (Eugene, OR: Wif and Stock, 2004), 22–23: "[There] were breaches of the first Commandment, such as the worship of Ashtoreth, Chemosh and Molech (1 Kings 11:1–8), and by Rehoboam, who sanctioned the consecration of prostitutes to serve in sacred worship (1 Kings 14:23, 24)."

[35] Herodotus. *Histories* 3.38.

[36] Genesis 1:27; Diels-Kranz, *Die* Fragmente der Vorsokratiker, Xenophanes frr. 15–16.

osophical" view of God, that is, "as One, ineffable and invisible, who could not be represented in images."[37] (Diodorus Siculus 40.3.4; Strabo 16.2.35)

During the late Hellenistic period, Jesus and his followers acknowledged the first commandment by affirming the worship of one God. Jesus famously taught, "I am the way and the truth and the life. No one comes to the Father except through me" (John 14:6). Later he referred to himself as the great "I Am" in John 8. The apostle Paul later preached the good news in Athens by teaching the polytheistic, pantheistic yet agnostic Athenian philosophers about the "unknown God" in Acts 17. When Christianity gradually took hold in the Mediterranean in later antiquity, some early Christians demonstrated their mental devotion to God through the formulation of the creeds or articulations of belief in one God. In time, later creeds, known as the Nicaean Creed and the Athanasian Creed, attempted to harmonize contentious viewpoints in order to promote worship of only one God who had three emanations that were manifest in simultaneous unified and orthodox, yet mysterious manner.

Often, however, throughout biblical history, God's people did not seem to trust or love him. Jeremiah taught the principle that anyone who trusted mankind "or trusted in the arm of flesh" was cursed (Jeremiah 17:5). The well-to-do often trusted in themselves because of a strong city (Proverbs 10:15) or a wedge of gold (Job 31:24) or even their own wisdom (Jeremiah 9:23).[38] While many in the Hebrew Bible did not trust God, by New Testament times, others were characterized as "lovers of pleasures more than lovers of God" (2 Timothy 3:4). More specifically, some loved ancient banqueting, and when anyone loves their belly more than God, he or she makes a god of it—"whose god is their belly"(Philippians 3:19). Many non-Israelites of the larger Mediterranean world were focused on finding pleasure and seeking fame, money, and power that became their gods.

---

[37] *Voluntary Associations in the Greco-Roman World.* Ed. John S. Kloppenborg and Stephen G. Wilson (New York: Routledge, 1996), 41.

[38] See a long discussion of this topic in Thomas Watson's *The Ten Commandments.* Grand Rapids, MI: Christian Classics Ethereal Library (First published as a part of *A Body of Practical Divinity,* 1692), 56.

The Ten Commandments have also played a significant role in teaching God's will throughout later Christian history. St. Augustine quoted the Decalogue to establish divine law in order to convict humankind of sin as well as teach both Israel and the Church the will of God.[39] During the early Middle Ages, some Eastern Byzantine Christians invoked a very literal interpretation of this commandment to justify defacing paintings, called icons, depicting God, Mary, and saints.[40] Later, reformers posed questions such as "What do you trust? Where do you turn in times of trouble?" Martin Luther answered, "Whatever thy heart clings to and relies upon, that is properly thy God."[41] Luther argued that sacred art was appropriate in church; indeed, he argued that to destroy it meant that it had power when it really had none. Luther believed that sacred art witnessed to the beauty of God's creation and was a powerful reminder of the biblical story by pointing out Moses's brazen serpent or Paul's disregard for Athens' idols.[42] In contrast to Luther's indifference toward art, the Swiss reformer Ulrich Zwingli waged war on idols in the interiors of churches while John Calvin was even more suspicious of the visual arts. Calvin believed that paying undue attention to physical, visible objects could obscure the worship of God "in spirit and in truth." Calvin believed that imagery in relation to the divine was best restricted to words, where it could be as extravagant or as startling as one pleased but whose interpretation did not bend toward the sin of idolatry.[43] The reformer John Calvin wrote, "When the people of Israel are faithful to the God of the covenant, then God has the right kind of representative in the world of humankind."[44] Beginning with

---

[39] Augustine *On the Spirit* 23-31 as quoted in *I am the Lord Your God: Christian Reflections on the Ten Commandments* edited by Carl E. Braaten and Christopher R. Seitz (Grand Rapids: Eerdmans, 2008), 13.

[40] Brown, Peter. *The Rise of Western Christendom* (Oxford: Blackwell, 1997), 238.

[41] Martin Luther quoted in Maxie D. Dunnam, *Exodus,* The Communicator's Commentary (Waco, TX: Word, 1987), 253

[42] For the brazen serpent, see Numbers 21; for Athenian idols, see Acts 17; Diarmaid MacCulloch, *The Reformation* (New York: Penguin, 2005), 144.

[43] Diarmaid MacCulloch. *The Reformation* (New York: Penguin, 2005), 248–49.

[44] Calvin. *Institutes* 2.8. Walter Harrelson. *The Ten Commandments and Human Rights* (Philadelphia: Fortress, 1980), 65.

Calvin, the concept of idolatry gradually became more and more abstract. The Puritan Thomas Watson wrote, "To trust in anything more than God, is to make it a god."[45] In modern, secular times, commenting on the 1992 completed tour of the band U2, *Rolling Stone* magazine concluded, "Their message? Thou shalt not worship false idols, but who else is there?"[46] It seems just finding the Judeo-Christian God, never mind putting him first, has become a complicated and difficult endeavor. Nevertheless, followers of God, both Jews and Christians are traditionally expected to be proper examples to others by having no other gods before him.

Summary

When Israel struggled with worshipping only one God, various hardships and developments such as famine, war, and exile gradually led to the adoption of rational, Greek monotheistic thinking, which eventually molded the Judeo-Christian tradition into believing in one mysterious, benevolent, omnipresent, and omnipotent God. Sometimes this trend expresses itself today as Christian vs. the non-Christian or Jews and Christians striving to become a proper image of God.

How Committed Are Americans to Having No Other Gods?

Belief in God is the obvious place to start when it comes to understanding the extent to which Americans are keeping the first commandment. If people do not even believe God exists, then they cannot have him in their lives at all, let alone make worshipping him a priority. To tackle this commandment, we analyzed data from

---

[45] Thomas Watson. *The Ten Commandments* (1692; repr. Edinburg: Banner of Truth, 1965), 55.

    Philip Graham Ryken *Written in Stone: The Ten Commandments and Today's Moral Crisis* (Phillipsburg, NJ: P&R Publishing, 2010, 66.

[46] *Rolling Stone*, 10–24 December 1992, 39] Michael S. Horton *The Law of Perfect Freedom* (Chicago: Moody, 2004), 17.

the General Social Survey (GSS), which is nationally recognized as a premier source of social science data.[47] About every other year since 1972, researchers have gathered data from thousands of Americans to create a dataset specifically designed to reflect the characteristics of the whole nation, and that can be used to look at specific religious, political, and cultural trends over time.

Survey respondents were asked, "Which statement comes closest to expressing what [they] believe about God?" Some clear and interesting trends emerge when we compare answers given to this question in 1988 to the answers given in 2016 (see Figure 1.1). First, there seems to be a downward trajectory in the percentage of people who "know God exists." During the almost thirty-year span represented, the number who "know" decreased from 64% to about 57%. There also seems to be a slight drop in the number of people who believe in God "with doubts" and believe in him "sometimes." Compared to the other three categories, these first three represent some degree of faith in an actual god-being, which could be considered the most traditional Judeo-Christian view of God. Ultimately, over 75% of Americans still express some level of belief in or knowledge of a God, but the confidence with which that faith is expressed and the number who express it has declined over the past three decades.

---

[47] Smith, Tom W, Peter Marsden, Michael Hout, and Jibum Kim. General Social Surveys, 1972-2016 [machine-readable data file] /Principal Investigator, Tom W. Smith; Co-Principal Investigator, Peter V. Marsden; Co-Principal Investigator, Michael Hout; Sponsored by National Science Foundation. -NORC ed.- Chicago: NORC at the University of Chicago [producer and distributor].

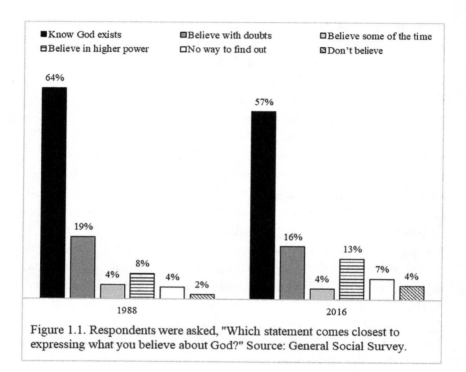

Figure 1.1. Respondents were asked, "Which statement comes closest to expressing what you believe about God?" Source: General Social Survey.

Inversely, an increasing number of Americans seem to be placing themselves in the three categories that represent less faith in the existence of God. Overall, an additional 5% of Americans believe in a less personal "higher power" compared to 1988, and as of 2016, 11% of individuals claim either no belief in God or think there is no way to know if there is a God. Notably, the number of atheists has more than doubled since 1988, and this group now comprises over 4% of all Americans (see Figure 1.1).

Most Americans believe in a god, but is it the God of the Judeo-Christian tradition? Figure 1.2 examines American religious preferences since 1980. It contains some striking patterns. First and foremost, it is notable that a high percentage of Americans continue to be Christian (nearly 73%), with another 2% identifying as Jewish, while the number of Protestants has declined sharply, from about 64% of the population to roughly 47%.

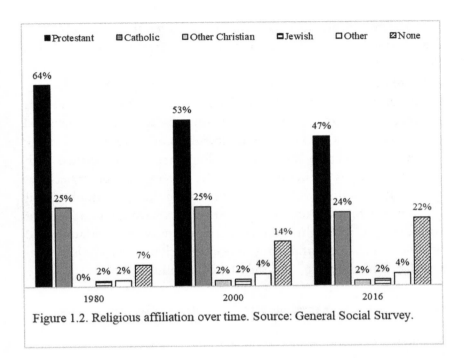

Figure 1.2. Religious affiliation over time. Source: General Social Survey.

By far, the most distinct trend is the rapid rise of the non-affiliated. While only 7% of the population considered themselves unaffiliated with religion in 1980, that percentage had more than tripled by 2016 (Figure 1.2). This growing number of "nones," as they are often called (and if you don't spell it out for them, it's always fun to tell people about the characteristics of the "nones"), signals a significant change in the American religious landscape, but it is hard to know what it says about the first commandment. In fact, further analysis reveals that the majority of "nones" continue to pray and engage in other types of religious activities.[48] Still, compared to the past, Americans are more disconnected from organized religion, and significantly fewer are affiliated with groups in the Judeo-Christian tradition.

---

[48] Smith, Tom W, Peter Marsden, Michael Hout, and Jibum Kim. General Social Surveys, 1972–2016 [machine-readable data file] /Principal Investigator, Tom W. Smith; Co-Principal Investigator, Peter V. Marsden; Co-Principal Investigator, Michael Hout; Sponsored by National Science Foundation. NORC ed. Chicago: NORC at the University of Chicago [producer and distributor].

Figure 1.3 provides us with another interesting way to examine adherence to the first commandment. Using the Baylor Religion Survey conducted in 2005 and then again in 2010,[49] we can explore the confidence Americans have in the existence of God and the ultimate truthfulness of their own religion by denomination. While the number of respondents for some groups is quite small, we included only those groups who had twenty members or more respond to the survey. Consequently, the corresponding data should be used with caution. Still, it is fascinating to note the extreme variability between groups. For example, 92% of Baptists claim to have "no doubts" that God exists while just under a quarter of Jews have the same level of confidence. One might wonder at the cause of this variation and whether it has implications for how effectively each group is at convincing its members to keep the first commandment.

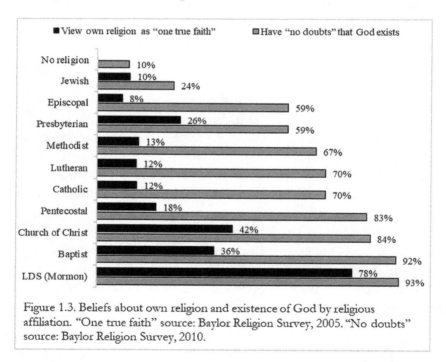

Figure 1.3. Beliefs about own religion and existence of God by religious affiliation. "One true faith" source: Baylor Religion Survey, 2005. "No doubts" source: Baylor Religion Survey, 2010.

[49] Baylor University. 2005 and 2010. *The Baylor Religion Survey*. Waco, TX: Baylor Institute for Studies of Religion [producer].

Likewise, it seems striking to see such a high percentage of religious adherents unwilling to claim their own religion as the right one (Figure 1.3). In fact, the majority of members of almost all groups do not consider their own denomination "the one true faith that leads to salvation," seemingly allowing for others to find God differently. It is possible, and even likely, that at least among Christians, people feel comfortable supporting various forms of Christianity since the Bible and Christ are the focus. Still, one cannot help but wonder if some of these patterns reflect willingness or the lack thereof to put their own perspective of God ahead of the perspectives of others. On a related note, in 2011 when directly asked whether "right and wrong should be based on God's laws" or "the views of society," 66% of Americans agreed that God's laws are the source of moral truth while a third believed the views of society should be the basis of right and wrong.[50]

While religious affiliation, belief in God, and looking to God as a source of truth are solid indicators of the status of the first commandment in the United States, it might be helpful to examine more deeply the degree to which people put God first in their lives. Obviously, it is easy to say one believes, but it is an entirely different thing to do something about it by practicing one's belief system. Of course, throughout this book, we will look at many different examples of adherence to religious doctrines and principles. For, now, we will look at prayer. The act of prayer would seem to indicate a deeper connection to and greater focus on God. It is well known that fewer people pray than claim to believe in God or a higher power. In fact, our analysis revealed that in 2016, nearly a third of Americans prayed "several times a day," while another third reported praying "once a day." Only about 15% of survey respondents reported they never pray. Praying seems to be a fixture of American culture, and the majority are praying to the Judeo-Christian God.

One last aspect of putting God first gleaned from the historical context relates to being an example of a believer by loving

---

50 Putman, Robert D., and David E. Campbell. 2011. Faith Matters Survey. The Association of Religion Data Archives [distributor]. http://www.thearda.com/Archive/Files/Descriptions/FTHMAT11.asp.

your neighbor. A few intriguing questions were asked on the Faith Matters Survey in 2011 that address this.[51] Respondents were asked whether they agree with the following statements: "Personally assisting people in trouble is very important to me." The vast majority of individuals (95%) agreed that assisting people in trouble is important to them, but significantly fewer (82%) gave any money to charitable or religious causes in the twelve months prior to answering the question. The majority of those reported giving away $500 or less in the previous year. Of course, charitably giving money is not the only way to love a neighbor, but it does make it clear that most Americans are trying to put at least a little money where their mouth is.

There are many other ways we could examine adherence to the first commandment, but the above information provides a good start. At the end of the day, the ultimate test of whether or not Americans have other gods is whether or not they keep all the commandments given by God. A God who is a priority would be obeyed. Consequently, the rest of the book collectively provides a more complete answer to the question of whether Americans keep this commandment. At this point, we encourage readers to refrain from judging compliance to it until they have carefully studied the evidence related to the other nine.

---

[51] Putman, Robert D., and David E. Campbell. 2011, Faith Matters Survey. The Association of Religion Data Archives [distributor]. http://www.thearda.com/Archive/Files/Descriptions/FTHMAT11.asp.

COMMANDMENT 2

"Thou shalt not make unto thee any graven image"

One reason that idolatry is not permitted in ancient Israel is because God wanted a people in the world that would serve only him and would be able to represent his cause to the world (Exodus 4:22–23). Restrictions and limits were imposed upon Israel's worship from the beginning as Israel represented Yahweh in the world. Also, Yahweh was "a jealous God." The Hebrew stem *k-n-'* usually rendered as *jealous* seems to have originally denoted becoming "intensely red." Because extreme and intense emotions affect facial coloration, the term came, by extension, to express ardor, zeal, rage, and jealousy and is only used to describe God, who is not indifferent to his creatures and is deeply involved in human affairs.[52] The human being, both male and female, was made in God's image and so likenesses of other creatures were discouraged. Forms of human beings or animals were not to be set up on pedestals at ritual sites or temples. Instead, living human beings were expected to do God's will and become testimonies "to the active presence and power of God in the world."[53] This commandment raises the topic of creation because it stressed that the creator should be worshiped. To make this point, the prophet

---

[52] Nahum M. Sarna. *The JPS Torah Commentary: Exodus* (New York: JPS, 1991), 110.
[53] Walter Harrelson. *The Ten Commandments and Human Rights* (Philadelphia: Fortress, 1980), 67.

Hosea notably mocked the worship of man-made idols: "The work-man made it: therefore it is not God" (8:6).[54] The common Hebrew adjective *pesel*, which describes an idol, means carved or hewed out. The "statue (*pesel*)" is the material object, the "image" (*temunāh*)" is its shape. *Pesel* typically describes a human creation and probably refers to an image of stone or wood overlaid with silver or gold.[55] However, vertical forms of worshipping Jehovah involved prayer and sacrifice whereas idolatry typically was easy, horizontal, permissive, and stressed human ingenuity.[56]

A wide range of activities were considered idolatrous in the Judeo-Christian tradition. Later Israelite prophets considered the following practices idolatrous: "the custom of kissing idols or images (Hosea 13:2; 1 Kings 19:18); of clothing them in costly garments (Ezekiel 16:18; Jeremiah 10:9); of offering incense to them (Ezekiel 8:11); [of kneeling] and prostrations before them (Deuteronomy 4:19; Isaiah 44:15; Jeremiah 8:2); of embracing anointing or wash-ing them (Mishnah Sanhedrin 7.6); of carrying them in procession (Isaiah 46:1, 7; Jeremiah 10:5)" and worshipping in a pagan tem-ple (2 Kings 5:18).[57] It is only fitting for worshippers to bow down to Yahweh, the true God (Genesis 24).[58] Surviving Jewish paintings at Dura-Europos of the third century CE demonstrate that it was

---

[54] Calum M. Carmichael. *The Ten Commandments* (Oxford: The Ninth Sacks Lecture, 1983), 19–20.

[55] Solomon Goldman. *The Ten Commandments* (Chicago: University of Chicago Press, 1956), 139. In Isaiah, XXX, 22, et al. It is used here because the com-mandment is addressed to the individual, who is normally too poor to make a *masechah* or molten image, like, for example, the golden calf, which was a cooperative effort. Although it may be applied to any kind of image, here it most probably refers to a human likeness, since every other thing is included in what follows.

[56] William H. C. Propp. *Exodus 19–40 The Anchor Bible* (New York: Doubleday, 2006), 169–70.

[57] R. H. Charles *The Decalogue* (Eugene, OR: Wif and Stock, 2004), 31; See also Mark F. Rooker *The Ten Commandments: Ethics for the 21st Century* (Nashville: B&H, 2010), 40.

[58] Mark F. Rooker. *The Ten Commandments: Ethics for the 21st Century* (Nashville: B&H, 2010), 40.

acceptable to some Jewish groups in later Roman times to paint figures representing prophets in religious scenes.[59]

This commandment famously became a point of friction in New Testament times between Jesus, his followers, and their envious critics as described in Christian sources. In Matthew 22:19, the coin Jesus asks his opponents to produce is the "coin used for the tax," a Roman denarius, which had on it not only Caesar's likeness but also the inscription "Tiberius Caesar, Augustus, son of divine Augustus" (see v. 20). In their concern for Torah practice—"Is it lawful . . ." equals "It is in line with Torah . . ."—Jesus's opponents are thus embarrassed by their possession of an unholy Roman coin. If, as is likely, it was the Herodians who had the incriminating coin, they would immediately have set themselves at odds with the subject Jewish population, which often opposed Roman rule. Followers of the Pharisees avoided all contact with such an idolatrous object. Thus, by the clever strategy of asking that the offensive coin be produced, Jesus has set his two groups of opponents against each other."[60] After Jesus's resurrection, Luke (in Acts 19:27) characterized silversmiths who crafted idols as greedily concerned about astronomical amounts of wealth, the survival of their traditional profession and their anxiety about the survival of Diana's temple and worship instead of worshipping God. These motives led to extralegal conflict with Paul's gospel message. Certainly, idolatry as characterized in the Judeo-Christian and Islamic traditions permeated much of ancient society—and this commandment sought to eradicate all forms of it.

Much later, in early modern times, this commandment was often quoted to reform the church or the larger society as a whole. For reform-minded people in Zurich, Switzerland, statues and paintings of saints and religious relics were considered idolatrous. Protestant Christians during the Reformation often defaced statues, threw whitewash on the paintings, and destroyed holy relics. The behavior,

---

[59] Henry Chadwick. *The Church in Ancient Society: From Galilee to Gregory the Great* (Oxford: Oxford University Press, 2003), 276.

[60] Bruce J. Malina and Richard L. Rohrbaugh. *Social-Science Commentary on the Synoptic Gospels* 2nd Edition (Minneapolis: Fortress Press, 2003), 112.

as seen through the eyes of the participants, was merely a logical extension of Ulrich Zwingli's (1484–1531) teachings.[61] Sir Francis Bacon (1561–1626) wrote, "There are four classes of idols which beset men's minds. To these, for distinction's sake, I have assigned names—calling the first class *Idols of the Tribe:* the second, *Idols of the Cave;* the third, *Idols of the Market-Place*; the fourth, *Idols of the Theatre.*"[62] In the modern Catholic tradition Pope Benedict XVI has argued that "when God made himself visible in Christ through the Incarnation, it became legitimate to reproduce the face of Christ" which helps teach everyone to see God.[63] Today believers in God could argue there is a much greater proliferation of potential idolatrous material and even more virtual objects to be worshipped than in any other time.

Summary

Clearly, making an idol was misguided because it mocked God's creation, and it became a means to serving other gods and the sinful lifestyle associated with them. By eschewing idolatry, God's followers could submit their will to his. Idolatry, as understood in the Judeo-Christian tradition, also led to abhorrent practices and often resulted in the financial exploitation of the less fortunate.

How Committed Are Americans to Not Making Idols?

As might be expected, data related to worshipping actual hand-carved idols is nonexistent. It may be that a statistically undetectable number of Americans worship physical objects in the place of supernatural deities. One might even be tempted to consider Christians' use of the cross or the presence of iconic depictions of saints used in

---

[61] David M Whitford. *A Reformation Life: The European Reformation through the Eyes of Philipp of Hesse* (Santa Barbara: Praeger, 2015), 71.

[62] Francis Bacon. *Novum Organum*, Aphorism I] Michael S. Horton *The Law of Perfect Freedom* (Chicago: Moody, 2004), 49.

[63] Pope Benedict XVI. *Great Christian Thinkers* (Minneapolis: Fortress, 2011), 172–173.

prayers as idols, but in such cases, religious adherents do not consider it a form of worshipping the actual object or even what it represents. Even if they did, we found no data to analyze on the prevalence of such practices. Consequently, we had to think more broadly about what might constitute bowing down to false idols in today's world. Since the origin of the commandment is a direct attempt to keep worshipers focused on the One True God, any object, entity, or person that receives attention or focus over God might be considered an idol. Ultimately, worship is about what or who people are devoted to.

A quick glance at the list of the top 20 most followed Twitter accounts is an interesting place to start our discussion of idolatry. We hope readers will appreciate this comparison as a point of interest even though we would hesitate to claim it is a direct measure of adherence to the second commandment. It should also be kept in mind that we did not isolate followers in the United States, so these Twitter numbers extend beyond just Americans. Clearly, actors, musicians, and other celebrities dominate the Twitterverse. This trend is not limited to just the top 20 either. At the very top is singer Katy Perry with well over 100 million followers, and rounding out the top 20 is Donald J. Trump, President of the United States, with almost 45 million followers (see Table 2.1). For comparison purposes, topping the list of Christian and Jewish religious leaders is Pope Francis. Though he serves at the head of well over 1 billion Catholics worldwide, including over 70 million in the United States, he only has 15,611,017 followers and ranks 129th on Twitter, not even outperforming MTV, which boasts 15.9 million followers.[64] Some other notable religious figures in the United States who do well on Twitter include Joel Osteen, a popular televangelist, with about 7.5 million Twitter followers, and Joyce Meyer, who runs a successful Christian ministry, and has over 5.5 million followers. Clearly, their numbers are dwarfed by many politicians, media outlets, singers, movie stars, and other famous entertainers.[65]

---

[64] Twittercounter.com. Retrieved on December 14, 2017 (https://twittercounter.com/pages/100)

[65] Twitter.com. Retrieved on December 14, 2017 (https://twitter.com/?lang=en)

Table 2.1. Most Followed Twitter Accounts Globally

Rank	User	# of Followers
1	Katy Perry	107,554,659
2	Justin Bieber	104,428,025
3	Barack Obama	97,893,676
4	Taylor Swift	85,798,611
5	Rihanna	84,318,554
6	Ellen DeGeneres	76,388,429
7	Lady Gaga	75,146,928
8	YouTube	70,672,154
9	Cristiano Ronaldo	66,198,444
10	Justin Timberlake	64,419,834
11	Twitter	62,212,850
12	Kim Kardashian West	57,681,432
13	Britney Spears	56,274,780
14	Ariana Grande	56,134,280
15	Selena Gomez	55,529,953
16	CNN Breaking News	53,738,770
17	Demi Lovato	53,021,834
18	Jimmy Fallon	50,004,928
19	Shakira	49,891,571
20	Donald J. Trump	44,704,165

Source: Twittercounter.com. Retrieved on December 14, 2017 (https://twittercounter.com/pages/100)

The most monitored individuals on Twitter have a number of devotees that far exceeds the most followed religious denominations in the United States. Outside of Catholicism, the Southern Baptist Convention is the largest denomination in America claiming 15,216,978 members,[66] while the National Baptist Convention

---

[66] sbc.net. Retrieved on December 15, 2017 (http://www.sbc.net/fastfacts/)

ranks third with an estimated 7.5 million members.[67] The fourth largest denomination is the United Methodist Church, which reports just over 7 million members,[68] and The Church of Jesus Christ of Latter-day Saints (Mormons) rounds out the top 5 claiming a membership of almost 6.6 million in the United States.[69] Please keep in mind that here we have related the membership numbers reported by each respective denomination rather than self-reported membership of individuals themselves. This invariably means these membership numbers are inflated, but we hope the point is still clear. Collectively, over 70% of the adult population in the United States self-identifies as Christian, which adds up to about 235 million Americans (including children). To provide some perspective, Katy Perry has almost half as many followers worldwide on Twitter as Christianity has adherents in the United States.

Of course, following someone or something on Twitter takes little effort and may reflect minimal dedication on the part of the follower. This might in some ways be comparable to the comfortable lifestyle of ancient idolatry. Consequently, we thought an examination of what Americans spend their time and money on would be even more relevant to this commandment. The Bureau of Labor Statistics conducts a study specifically designed to determine how people spend their time. The American Time Use Survey (ATUS) has been completed every year since 2003 and has collected data from over 180,000 individuals ages fifteen and older during that time. Because techniques were used to collect information from a sampling of Americans that had characteristics consistent with the whole population, we are quite confident these numbers closely match the numbers we would get if all Americans were surveyed. Selected respondents were interviewed in-depth and asked to report exactly how they used their time from 4:00 a.m. the day prior to the

---

[67] nationalbaptist.com. Retrieved on December 15, 2017 (http://www.national-baptist.com/about-us/index.html)

[68] umc.org. Retrieved on December 15, 2017 (http://www.umc.org/news-and-media/united-methodists-at-a-glance)

[69] mormonnewsroom.org. Retrieved on December 14, 2017 (https://www.mormonnewsroom.org/facts-and-statistics/country/united-states)

interview until 4:00 a.m. the day of the interview. They were specifically directed *not* to describe their "usual" day, but instead to break down the details of the actual day in question. The researchers used accepted analytical procedures to ensure that each day of the week and each month of the year is appropriately represented by the data, so all the numbers presented should provide a good sense of how typical Americans spend their time. A time-use diary of each hour and minute of the twenty-four-hour period was constructed, and the reported averages will be examined here.[70]

Not surprisingly, people spend the most amount of their time doing necessary things such as sleeping and working. But outside of these required activities, how do they spend their time? We will specifically focus on time spent engaged in leisure activities because that is time that surely could be used differently based on what a person values. The data reveal that the amount of time spent on the top two types of leisure (watching TV and socializing) has remained fairly steady over the past twelve years. While there are some minor ups and downs, there is nothing to suggest a clear trend toward or away from any of the activities included in our analysis. As Figure 2.1 shows, watching TV dominates the leisure time of Americans, the average person watching close to three hours per day. The next most prevalent leisure activity is socializing, but it only garners about a fourth of the attention that TV watching does (39 minutes). In addition, the average American spends about fourteen minutes a day playing games, ten minutes using a computer for leisure, seventeen minutes reading for personal interest, and almost twenty minutes participating in sports, exercise, and recreation. Overall, the average American commits over five hours of their day to engaging in leisure and sports activities. When compared to leisure, Americans spend very little time engaging in religious and spiritual activities or volunteering. In fact, on average, Americans reported spending less than ten minutes of their day on religion and even less time (eight

---

[70] Bureau of Labor Statistics. 2017. "American Time Use Survey User's Guide". Retrieved January 27, 2018 (https://www.bls.gov/tus/atususersguide.pdf).

minutes) volunteering. Combined, this amounts to one-tenth of the time the average person spent watching television (see Figure 2.1).

If we remove from the analysis people who did not even attempt to do each activity, the differences are not as dramatic. Of the individuals who reported watching some television, the average amount of time spent was just under three and a half hours. Likewise, the numbers increase to over two hours a day for games and about 1.5 hours each for leisurely computer use, reading, and sports and recreation. For those who chose to engage in religious and spiritual activities on the day about which the data was collected, over 1.5 hours was spent on it, and those who volunteered did so for over two hours on the day in question. Clearly, individuals who take time to engage in these activities, spend significant time on them, but even then the focus on spiritual and religious endeavors is dwarfed by the attention the average American gives to leisure (Figure 2.2).

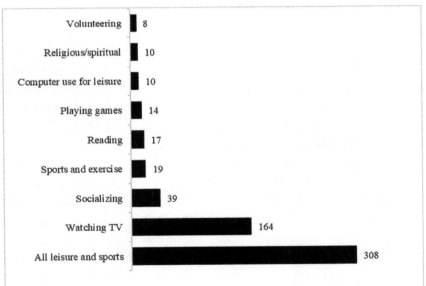

Figure 2.1. Average minutes per day spent engaging in religious, leisure, and volunteer activities (including all surveyed). Source: American Time Use Survey, 2016.

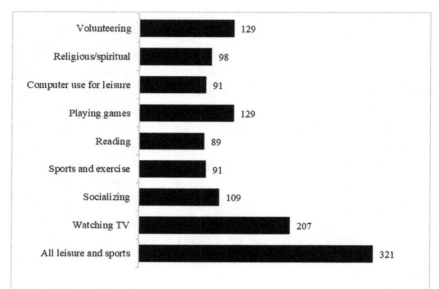

Figure 2.2. Average minutes per day spent engaging in religious, leisure, and volunteer activities (including only those who participate in each activity). Source: American Time Use Survey, 2016.

While it seems recreation and leisure dominate the disposable time of Americans, there are a few other measures we can examine to determine how much focus people are giving to God and religion. Figure 2.3 presents data taken from the 2010 Baylor Religion Survey, which asked 1,714 participants a series of questions related to their religious participation during the past month. It is evident that the majority of Americans do not spend their time participating in church social gatherings, religious education programs, or Bible study, nor do they attempt to share their faith with others (Figure 2.3). When asked about the frequency of reading their sacred book in private, 29% reported never doing it and only 32% responded they read it weekly or more. The majority of individuals who read a sacred book only did so several times a year or less.[71]

---

[71] Baylor University. 2010. *The Baylor Religion Survey, Wave III*. Waco, TX: Baylor Institute for Studies of Religion [producer].

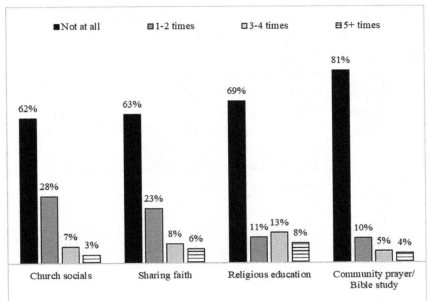

Figure 2.3. Frequency of participation in religion-oriented activities in the last month. Source: Baylor Religion Survey, 2010.

Just as the way we spend our time reflects our devotions, so too does how we spend our money. The United States Bureau of Labor Statistics 2016 Consumer Expenditure Survey provides a detailed breakdown of American spending. It will surprise few that when it comes to the total of all household expenditures made, the majority of Americans are spending over 80% of what they make on housing (33%), transportation (16%), food (13%), insurance (12%) and healthcare (8%). Outside of these more essential categories, the next highest type of expenditure for Americans is entertainment. In fact, the survey found that just over 5% of expenditures people made were for entertainment, a number that has remained fairly steady for several decades. The average household spent about $3,000 on fun, including $681 on fees and admissions, $1,085 on audio and visual equipment and services, $740 on pets, toys, hobbies, and playground equipment, and $406 on other entertainment products.[72]

Comparatively, only 21% of Americans surveyed in 2010, who reported attending a place of worship, contributed more than $3,000 to their church. If we include all Americans, even those who reported having no place of worship in the past year, only about 11% of households gave more to a religious cause than they spent on entertainment. Indeed, the majority of self-identified religious adherents (57%) donated less than $1,000 in tithes and offerings to their church (see Figure 2.4).[73]

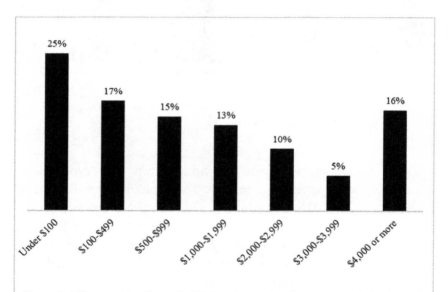

Figure 2.4. Percentage of households that donated each amount to their place of worship in the last year (includes only those with a place of worship). Source: Baylor Religion Survey, 2010.

---

[72] U.S. Bureau of Labor Statistics. 2016 *Consumer Expenditure Survey*. Retrieved December 19, 2017 (https://www.bls.gov/cex/)

[73] Baylor University. 2010. *The Baylor Religion Survey, Wave III*. Waco, TX: Baylor Institute for Studies of Religion [producer].

More generally speaking, a report by The Giving Institute found that charities received over $390 billion from Americans in 2016. Slightly more than 72% of that was given by individuals while the remaining amount was donated by foundations, corporations, or by bequest. Almost $123 billion was received by religious groups, the largest of any category of recipients, the next being education at almost $60 billion.[74] In contrast, the United States entertainment market was valued at almost $600 billion in 2014 and is estimated to be nearing almost $700 billion at the close of 2017.[75]

Clearly, Americans spend a lot of time and money seeking entertainment while considerably less seems to be focused on their spiritual and religious pursuits. How much does a devotee need to do and spend to claim a sufficient focus on worshipping God over alternative pursuits or idols? Ponder that question for a few minutes as we turn to a discussion of taking the Lord's name in vain.

---

[74] *Giving USA 2017: The Annual Report on Philanthropy for the Year 2016*, a publication of Giving USA Foundation, 2017, researched and written by the Indiana University Lilly Family School of Philanthropy. Available online at www.givingusa.org.

[75] Afroprofile. (n.d.). Value of the entertainment and media market in the United States from 2011 to 2020 (in billion U.S. dollars). In *Statista - The Statistics Portal*. Retrieved December 16, 2017 (https://www.statista.com/statistics/237769/value-of-the-us-entertainment-and-media-market).

COMMANDMENT 3

"Thou shalt not take the name of the LORD thy God in vain"

The most common ways in which ancient Israelites took the Lord's name in vain was through swearing falsely when taking a vow or an oath or by using God's name in magic (Leviticus 19:12; Ps. 139:20). Certainly, by invoking the name of God, one could exploit God's power for any purpose, good or evil, or use his name to promote unwise or selfish practices. One commentator noted that "to know an entity's name is to possess power over it, as when the first Man names the animals and Woman (Genesis 2:19, 23) and he later renames her Eve (Genesis 3:20). Moses had early on asked to know Yahweh's name (Exodus 3:13), a request that the Deity evidently finds threatening. By continually revealing his true name to Israel, Yahweh makes himself vulnerable."[76] Why would a deity become so vulnerable in revealing his name? "Because giving a name, knowing a name, and using a name are expressions of control. In folkloric magic in many cultures, when divine beings were called upon by their proper names, they were compelled to act. In the Bible, when the first human named the animals, he showed his dominion over them (Genesis 2:19–20; compare 1:28). When foreign rulers appointed kings over Judah, they sometimes changed their clients'

---

[76] William H. C. Propp *Exodus 19-40 The Anchor Bible* (New York: Doubleday, 2006), 174.

names, showing them who was really in charge (see 2 Kings 23:34; 24:17)."[77]

Because of this sacred relationship with covenant Israel, if either a citizen of Israel or an alien blasphemed the name of the Lord, the people were to stone the violator to death (Leviticus 24:16). God wanted to make his name holy both among the Israelites and the nations of the world so it could not be profaned. (Ezekiel 39:7).[78]

In addition, the Hebrew expression *lassaw'* not only means to take something "in vain," but also to treat Yahweh's name lightly, to use it idly, or even to treat it with light contempt. Occasionally, Yahweh's name seems to have been misused to do harm, sometimes through magical means, to others. Ancient Israelites were reluctant to use God's personal name in their pronouncement of curses.[79] Job 1:5 and Job 2:9 denote swearing in vain which seem to mean "cursing God," which Job refuses to do and for which he is later greatly blessed. The third commandment forbade that religion should ever be used as a tool to manipulate, coerce, incite violence, or exploit others although it often has been used for precisely that in many times and places. The prophet Hosea (in 4:8) spoke about the priests who, instead of serving, "feed upon the sins of the people" and are "greedy for their iniquity".[80] Many ancient prophets rebuked priests for using religion for any kind of personal gain.

Philo emphasized the power of a deity's name in Roman times when he wrote that "the name always stands second to the thing which it represents, as the shadow which follows the body. After speaking first about the existence of the Ever-existent and the honor due to him as such, He follows it at once in orderly sequence by giving a commandment on the proper use of His title . . . An oath . . .

---

[77] Michael Coogan *The Ten Commandments: A Short History of An Ancient Text* (New Haven: Yale University Press, 2014), 66.

[78] Dan Lioy *The Decalogue in the Sermon on the Mount* Studies in Biblical Literature 66 (New York: Peter Lang, 2004), 64–5.

[79] Walter Harrelson *The Ten Commandments and Human Rights* (Philadelphia: Fortress, 1980), 73.

[80] Walter Harrelson. *The Ten Commandments and Human Rights* (Philadelphia: Fortress, 1980). 75.

is no small thing, though custom makes light of it. For an oath is an appeal to God as a witness on matters in dispute, and to call Him as witness to a lie is the height of profanity."[81] Philo also praised the Essenes, a Jewish ascetic desert community, because they avoided swearing, and regarded it as "worse than perjury; for they say that he who cannot be believed without swearing by God is already condemned."[82] In the New Testament, seven sons of Sceva were beaten and driven away by an evil spirit (Acts 19:13–16) when they used the Lord's name without being his devoted followers.

Various Gentile groups also taught the basic principles of the third commandment. The Greeks despised the frequent habit of swearing as they did perjury. In the Twelve Tables of Rome, it was directed that false witnesses be executed by being thrown from the Tarpeian Rock. The Persians refused to swear. The Scythians are said to have told Alexander the Great: "We swear only by keeping our word." An Arab proverb runs: "Never swear, but let your words be yes and no."[83]

Later in the Christian tradition, Jesus also emphasized that disciples should not swear at all (Matthew 5:34), but one should only say yes or no (5:37). Paul taught the principle that the gospel message involved simple statements of yes, which helped people avoid oaths (2 Cor. 1:19). Goethe, a nineteenth-century Romantic poet, critiqued the local clergy who had God's name "daily in their mouths, a mere phrase, a barren name, to which no thought is attached whatever. If they were impressed by His greatness, they would be dumb, and through veneration unwilling to name Him."[84]

---

[81] Philo. *Decalogue* 82-86 quoted in Solomon Goldman *The Ten Commandments* (Chicago: University of Chicago Press, 1956), 153–154.

[82] Philo. *de decem Orac.* 17 quoted in R. H. Charles The Decalogue (Eugene, OR: Wif and Stock, 2004), 93.

[83] Solomon Goldman. *The Ten Commandments* (Chicago: University of Chicago Press, 1956), 160.

[84] Eckermann. *Conversations with Goethe*, December 31, 1823 quoted in Solomon Goldman *The Ten Commandments* (Chicago: University of Chicago Press, 1956), 155.

Summary

This commandment underscores the significance of keeping one's oaths and using religion only for good, especially after forming a relationship with God. Those who are honest enough to make an oath should not need to make one at all. Often oaths have been used to manipulate, exploit others, or to commit or cover up crime, which not only denigrates God and his followers, but also demonstrates a lack of respect toward other human beings.

How Committed Are Americans to Not Taking the Name of God in Vain?

The death of Cardinal Bernard F. Law, who was in the middle of the Catholic priest abuse scandal, which embroiled the United States and the world, reminds us that religious adherents do not always live up to their own commitments to the teachings and standards of their professed faith. Cardinal Law resigned after it was discovered that he had been covering up for abusive priests for many years.[85] Religious leaders from Jimmy Swaggart to Ted Haggard have been in the public eye as they fell from the grace of their respective religious organizations because of moral failures. Of course, such incidents are not limited to high-profile believers. But how effectively do Americans conform to the standards of what they claim to believe?

Since the third commandment relates to how people use the name of God, it seems the focus of the data presented must be on individuals who personally claim to have taken that name upon themselves in the form of commitment to beliefs or a particular form of faith. We recognize many have made no commitments to Judeo-Christian ideals, and consequently, they cannot really take the Lord's name in vain or even use his name improperly because they did not claim loyalty to it in the first place. Thus, in this chapter, we will

---

[85] McFadden, Robert D. 2017. "Bernard Law, Powerful Cardinal Disgraced by Priest Abuse Scandal, Dies at 86." Retrieved December 21, 2017 (https://www.nytimes.com/2017/12/19/obituaries/cardinal-bernard-law-dead.html)

examine to what extent those who claim to be Bible-believing Jews or Christians actually follow the related teachings. This is the only chapter where we focus on compliance with Judeo-Christian commandments or teachings in the context of who should be keeping them, based on their own claims of belief or affiliation.

The result of our approach will be somewhat of a preview of parts of the rest of the book. However, we will not provide any totals here if they are presented elsewhere but instead will focus on the impact of belief and affiliation claims on compliance to some key measures of the other commandments. Essentially, the commandment not to take the Lord's name in vain is the only commandment that cannot be broken unless one has committed to believe and follow a biblical path. How well are believers conforming to the commandments and teachings presented in their own sacred texts?

In the 2016 General Social Survey, participants were asked, "Which of these statements comes closest to describing your feelings about the Bible?" The possible answers were "The Bible is the actual word of God and is to be taken literally, word for word," "The Bible is the inspired word of God, but not everything should be taken literally, word for word," or "The Bible is an ancient book of fables, legends, history, and moral precepts recorded by man." The Baylor Religion Survey in 2010 asked a similar question but gave slightly different answer options. Respondents could select "The Bible means exactly what it says. It should be taken literally, word-for-word, on all subjects," "The Bible is perfectly true, but it should not be taken literally, word-for-word, we must interpret its meaning," "The Bible contains some human error," or "The Bible is an ancient book of history and legends." It stands to reason that a person who provided the first answer to both of these questions should be most obligated to conforming to exactly what the Bible says, including the Ten Commandments, and the individuals giving the last answer would be much less likely to feel a sense of obligation to do anything the Bible commands.[86]

---

[86] Baylor University. 2010. *The Baylor Religion Survey, Wave III*. Waco, TX: Baylor Institute for Studies of Religion [producer].

Not surprisingly, a comparison between the groups reveals almost exactly what one might expect. Individuals who believe the Bible is a book of fables are among the least likely on every indicator to conform to commandment teachings while people who believe the Bible should be taken literally are the most conforming. Those who feel it is inspired or contains errors land somewhere in the middle. When we compare people affiliated with Christianity or Judaism to those who claim no religious affiliation, we discover the same predictable finding. Christians and Jews are more likely to be committed to the behaviors, attitudes, and beliefs connected to the traditions of their faiths.

While we find the disparities between Bible literalists and Bible rejecters and Judeo-Christians and the non-affiliated to be fascinating, we are not going to discuss them in any depth here. Instead, we encourage readers to spend some time digesting the information on their own. What might the implications be? Consistent with the third commandment, we will focus primarily on the first two columns of each table. How are self-reported, committed Bible believers and affiliated Jews and Christians doing when it comes to conforming to biblical doctrines?

Figure 3.1 provides some measures related to the having no other gods (first commandment), keeping the Sabbath day holy (fourth commandment), and the commandment not to kill (the sixth). Nearly 90% of respondents who profess to believe the Bible literally also claim to know God exists, and almost 85% of them pray at least once a day. Interestingly, those numbers drop down about 53% and 58% respectively for those who only view the Bible as inspired. The disparity in church attendance, related to keeping the Sabbath day holy, and abortion attitudes, which is often tied by Christians to killing, are even greater. Well, more than twice as many of the literalists (47% vs. 20%) attend church weekly, and they are half as likely as those who think the Bible is inspired to think abortion should be allowed for any reason (21% vs. 47%).

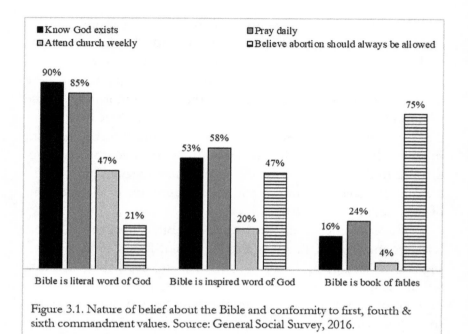

Figure 3.1. Nature of belief about the Bible and conformity to first, fourth & sixth commandment values. Source: General Social Survey, 2016.

When it comes to conformity to the commandment to avoid adultery, the pattern is the same (see Figure 3.2). Most respondents have never committed adultery, but fewer (14%) of those who take the Bible literally claimed to have done this. Please note, that one has no way of knowing when the adultery may have occurred or whether it was before or after survey participants came to accept the Bible literally. It is impossible to know with this measure if the commitment to God happened prior to going against the biblical teaching. When it comes to attitudes about sexuality, 90% of literalists believe extramarital sex is always wrong while 75% view homosexuality as always wrong. In contrast, among those who view the Bible as inspired, 78% think extramarital sex is always wrong and 30% feel the same way about homosexual sex. Bible literalists are 2.5 times more likely to take a definitive negative view of homosexuality. Finally, more than twice as many who accept an inspired Bible (5%) have had sex for pay in the past year than the 2% of the literalists. Interestingly, about the same percentage of Americans who see the Bible as fables had sex for pay (5%) as individuals who consider it inspired (see Figure 3.2).

An examination of Figure 3.3 reveals a majority of people who believe the Bible means exactly what it says focus time and money on their religious endeavors, which is a sign of having no other gods, the second commandment. Most shared their faith with others (69%), participated in religious education in the last month (62%) and donated at least $1,000 to their place of worship (57%). A minority of respondents who claimed to believe the Bible is true, but needs interpretation did the same (47%, 40%, and 48% respectively). Only 26% of individuals who believe the Bible contains human error shared their faith while 20% participated in religious education. Interestingly, almost twice as many in the same category (38%) donated at least $1,000 to their place of worship in the past year revealing a tendency of those with less faith in the Bible to be more willing to give money than time and effort to their religion.

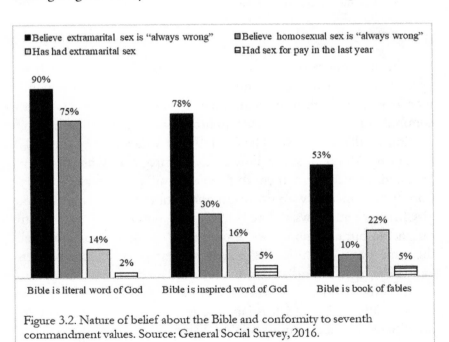

Figure 3.2. Nature of belief about the Bible and conformity to seventh commandment values. Source: General Social Survey, 2016.

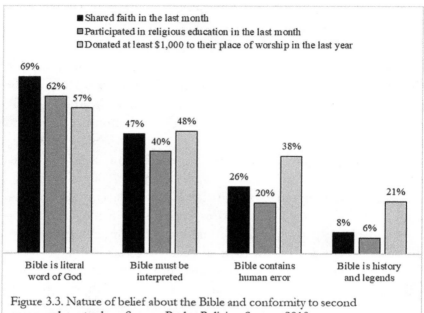

Figure 3.3. Nature of belief about the Bible and conformity to second commandment values. Source: Baylor Religion Survey, 2010.

In the absence of a specific measure related to Bible belief, we opted to consider the commands to honor parents (fifth commandment), not steal (eighth commandment), not bear false witness (ninth commandment), and not covet (tenth commandment) in light of religious affiliation claims. The 2011 World Values Survey and 2012 Measuring Morality Study allowed us to categorize Christians and Jews and then compare them to people claiming no religious affiliation. In conjunction with the commandment to honor parents, 83% of Christians and Jews claimed they would never curse their parent for any amount of money while only 62% of the non-religious felt the same way. A significantly higher percentage of religious adherents (80%) than unaffiliated individuals (69%) believe stealing property is never justified, and when it comes to avoiding fares on public transportation, 58% of Christians and Jews compared to 45% of the unaffiliated consider it unjustifiable (Figure 3.4).

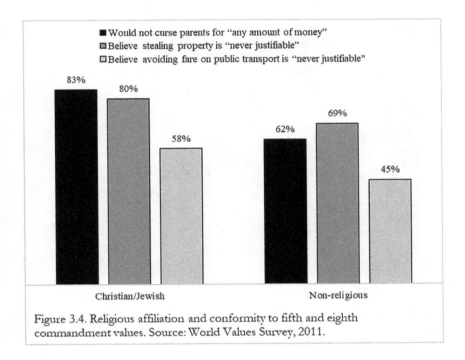

Figure 3.4. Religious affiliation and conformity to fifth and eighth commandment values. Source: World Values Survey, 2011.

In terms of honesty or bearing false witness, we find a similar pattern. Christians and Jews are considerably more likely to believe it is extremely immoral to lie to a teacher about a test score (43% vs. 26%) or fake an injury to collect insurance (74% vs. 57%). They are also more likely to say they would never cheat in a game of cards for any amount of money (63% vs. 49%). Finally, 27% of individuals who affiliate with Judaism and Christianity responded it is "sometimes" like them to "want to have a lot of money and expensive things," compared to 36% of the non-affiliated, which is our indicator of coveting, the tenth commandment (see Figure 3.5).

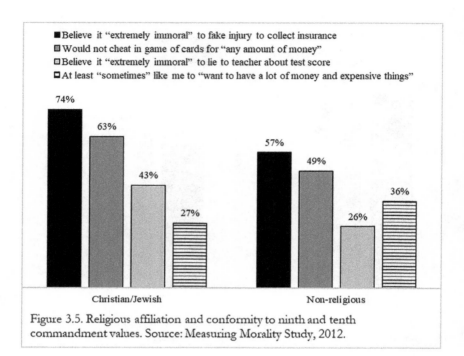

Figure 3.5. Religious affiliation and conformity to ninth and tenth commandment values. Source: Measuring Morality Study, 2012.

In almost all instances we examined, the majority of Bible literalists and Judeo-Christians seem to be conforming to teachings of the Ten Commandments. The only exceptions among our sampling of measures are that fewer than half attend church weekly and a minority believe it is extremely immoral to lie to a teacher about a test score. The level of conformity of the believers in an inspired Bible is considerably lower while those who view the Bible as a purely human construction are most likely to hold to values and beliefs that contradict the Decalogue. On any given indicator, a significant percentage of professed believers do not seem eager to accept attitudes and engage in behaviors demanded by their God through Bible teachings. Are there enough who do to conclude that overall America is doing a good job avoiding taking the Lord's name in vain? Consider that for a minute as we dig deeper into Sabbath Day observance in the United States.

COMMANDMENT 4

"Remember the sabbath day, to keep it holy"

Work and rest, both principles exemplified by God in the Garden of Eden, form the background to this commandment. The first man was placed in the garden to till and cultivate it (Genesis 2:15). The man named all the animals (Genesis 2:19–20), then greeted the gift of the woman shaped from his rib (Genesis 2:23). The couple came into being in order that each may contribute life to the other, that life may be shared, and that solitariness might be overcome. The man and woman were commanded to become fruitful and care for the earth. In the Hebrew creation narrative, work was not the primary reason "the human being was called into being," so there was also a time to rest.[87] The Hebrew imagery of a mighty hand moved by a still stretched-out arm described God's work to restore the created order found in the world—the pattern of hard labor for six days followed by a seventh day of rest. No definition of work is given here, but elsewhere in the Bible certain types of work are specified.[88] Michael Coogan noted that "the work not to be done on the Sabbath is specified—not carrying burdens, at least into Jerusalem (Jeremiah 17:21)—but never as systematically as later

---

[87] Walter Harrelson. *The Ten Commandments and Human Rights* (Philadelphia: Fortress, 1980), 85.

[88] Nahum M. Sarna. *The JPS Torah Commentary: Exodus* (New York: JPS, 1991), 112.

rabbinic commentators would elaborate. Mishnah Shabbat 7:2 lists thirty-nine categories of work, each defined in detail in what follows. Some of these are mentioned in the Bible: plowing and harvesting (Exodus 34:21; Mark 2:23–24); lighting a fire (Exodus 35:3); gathering wood (Numbers 15:32–36); doing business (Amos 8:5; Isaiah 58:13; Nehemiah 10:31). In some biblical passages, Sabbath violation is a capital crime, for which the punishment was death (see Exodus 31:14–15; Numbers 15:32–36)."[89]

The first Sabbath was observed by Yahweh himself (Genesis 2:2–3), and by resting one day a week, later generations could unite in imitation of God himself.[90] One might wonder how mankind could sanctify (Exodus 20:8, 11) that which God already accomplished and sanctified? More likely this commandment means to "treat the Sabbath as holy," like a sacrificial offering and a thing proper to the divine realm, not to be mingled with the profane.[91] The Hebrew root *zkr*, which is usually rendered as *remember*, implies not just recollection, but even action based upon memory. "For example, in [Exodus] 13:3 the command to 'remember' the Exodus from Egypt motivates the season's rituals. So too, remembering the Sabbath and the recollection of Yahweh's primordial rest should prompt one to abstain from work."[92]

By proscribing work and creativity on that day, and by enjoining the inviolability of nature one day a week, this commandment restores nature to its original state of human freedom. Human liberty is immeasurably enhanced, human equality is strengthened, and the use of social justice is promoted by legislating the inalienable right of every human being to one day of complete rest every seven days.[93] The account in Deuteronomy, "unlike the Exodus one, draws spe-

---

[89] Michael Coogan. *The Ten Commandments: A Short History of An Ancient Text* (New Haven: Yale University Press, 2014), 69–70.

[90] William H. C. Propp *Exodus 19–40 The Anchor Bible* (New York: Doubleday, 2006), 177.

[91] William H. C. Propp *Exodus 19–40 The Anchor Bible* (New York: Doubleday, 2006), 176.

[92] William H. C. Propp. *Exodus 19-40 The Anchor Bible* (New York: Doubleday, 2006), 175.

[93] Nahum M. Sarna *The JPS Torah Commentary: Exodus* (New York: JPS, 1991), 113.

cial attention to servants and their need for rest. The reason would appear to be the awareness that they might be made to work seven days a week. If so, it would be a further indication that the law-giver had this aspect of things in mind about the Israelites in Egypt. Noteworthy in this regard is the call to remember the bondage in Egypt follows immediately the instruction about the Israelite servants' need for rest."[94]

Some scholars have argued that rest on the Sabbath day was instituted later because, while in Babylon, Jews had learned to regard the number seven as sacred. A weekly day of rest had been observed during the harvest season (Exodus 34:21), as well as the Sabbatical every seventh year (Leviticus 21:3–4).[95] Sabbath is derived from *Shabbat*, which comes from the Hebrew *shbt*, meaning to "cease, desist, rest, repose" or possibly even the Assyrian *sabattu*, "keep a holiday," or "be free."[96] Even animals were prohibited from working (Deuteronomy 22:6–7, Deuteronomy 25:4). It became a breach of the Sabbath to light a fire (Exodus 35:3) or to bake bread or boil meat (16:23), and to gather sticks for such purposes (Numbers 15:32) was an offense punishable by death.[97] A few verses later (Numbers 15:35), a man who gathered sticks on the Sabbath was commanded to be stoned. The Sabbath Day granted leisure for people to reflect on God's great work of creation and His deliverance of His people. Children commonly heard about how the Lord fed Israel with manna, but it was not collected on the Sabbath (Exodus 16:26). The tradition of remembering the Sabbath Day separated Israel from its neighbors into a holy community. After suffering in captivity, God explained that this suffering was a consequence of their failure to keep the Sabbath holy (Jeremiah 17:19–27 and Ezekiel 20:12–13). For this reason, after Judah was taken into captivity, Nehemiah

[94] Calum M. Carmichael *The Ten Commandments* (Oxford: The Ninth Sacks Lecture, 1983), 21-22.

[95] Solomon Goldman *The Ten Commandments* (Chicago: University of Chicago Press, 1956), 162.

[96] Solomon Goldman *The Ten Commandments* (Chicago: University of Chicago Press, 1956), 166.

[97] R. H. Charles *The Decalogue* (Eugene, OR: Wipf and Stock, 2004), 124.

understood that keeping the fourth commandment was essential to public safety (Nehemiah 13:19).

Among the Jewish people, "the Sabbath was recognized as a day of rest from ordinary work, but still more as a holy day set apart for the building up of the spiritual element in man (Philo in *Eus. Praep. Evang.* 8.7; Josephus *Ant.* 16.2.4) for private prayer, meditation, and for public worship in the Synagogue (Mark 1:21, 23; Luke 4:31, 33, 6:6, 13:10; Acts 13:14, 43) or the Temple.[98] Even the hours preceding the Sabbath were accounted holy. On the eve of the Sabbath or the Day of Preparation (Mark 15:42; Matthew 26:62; Luke 23:54; Josephus *Ant.* 16.6.2) no business might be undertaken that might encroach on the Sabbath. Yet the Sabbath was not to be a fast but a feast day, as we learn from the Book of Judith (8:6). In Isaiah, the Sabbath was called a delight (58:13)."[99] Philo noted that "the Judeans every seventh day occupy themselves with the philosophy of their fathers, dedicating that time to the acquiring of knowledge and the study of the truths of nature. For what are our places of prayer . . . but schools of prudence and courage and temperance and justice"[100] (Philo *Eudaimonia*, 2.216). Jesus taught it was permissible to do good on the Sabbath when he posed the question: "Which one of you, if he has a sheep, and it falls into a pit on the Sabbath, will not grab hold of it and pull it out? How much more valuable is a person than a sheep! (Matthew 12:11–12)."[101]

For early Christians, observance of the Sabbath changed to Sunday beginning in New Testament times. Christ rose from the grave on the first day of the week and appeared twice on that day to his disciples (John 20:19, 26). The apostles had begun to meet and worship together and to break bread when Paul preached unto them to remember Christ's resurrection (Acts 20:7; 1 Corinthians 16:2). Jesus was established as the Lord of the Sabbath (Mark 2:28) and

---

[98] Philo in *Eus. Praep. Evang.* 8.7; Josephus *Ant.* 16.2.4.

[99] R. H. Charles. *The Decalogue* (Eugene, OR: Wif and Stock, 2004), 126.

[100] Voluntary Associations in the Greco-Roman World. Ed. John S. Kloppenborg and Stephen G. Wilson (New York: Routledge, 1996), 43.

[101] Michael Coogan *The Ten Commandments: A Short History of An Ancient Text* (New Haven: Yale University Press, 2014), 71–72.

the Sabbath became the Lord's Day (Revelation 1:10). However, one scholar argued that "never in the New Testament itself is [Sunday] equated with the Sabbath as a weekly day of rest.[102] Later church fathers wrote that Christians needed to keep no Sabbaths, but rather they should keep the Lord's Day as a memorial of the beginning of the new creation.[103] During the apostolic period, in his character-istic refusal to allow such things to become a basis for judging fel-low believers, Paul supported Christian Gentiles' freedom either to observe or not observe the Jewish Sabbath (Romans 14:5), but it still seems that, according to Luke, many had decided that worshipping on Sunday became more appropriate.[104] Sunday was made an official holy day for Christianity by the emperor Constantine in 321.[105] The Sabbath was firmly established on Sunday in Christendom during the medieval period up through the centuries of Reformation and Counter-Reformation and into the modern period. The Protestant Westminster Confession expressed that keeping the Sabbath holy was "a positive, moral, and perpetual commandment."[106] The Judeo-Christian tradition recently has influenced Western societies to have a modern weekend.

Summary

Remembering the Sabbath for ancient Israel entailed a com-plete cessation of all forms of work for humans of all ranks and even animals in order to remember God's creative work. Mankind was

---

[102] (1 Corinthians 16:2). Michael Coogan *The Ten Commandments: A Short History of An Ancient Text* (New Haven: Yale University Press, 2014), 73.

[103] Athanasius (*de Sabb. et circum.* 4); quoted in R. H. Charles *The Decalogue* (Eugene, OR: Wif and Stock, 2004), 139.

[104] Mark F. Rooker. *The Ten Commandments: Ethics for the 21st Century* (Nashville: B&H, 2010), 97.

[105] (1 Corinthians 16:2). Michael Coogan. *The Ten Commandments: A Short History of An Ancient Text* (New Haven: Yale University Press, 2014), 73.

[106] Westminster Confession XXI.7 quoted in Philip Graham Ryken *Written in Stone: The Ten Commandments and Today's Moral Crisis* (Phillipsburg, NJ: P&R Publishing, 2010, 111.

not just a working being, so he or she also needed time to reflect and learn about God.

How Committed Are Americans to Keeping the Sabbath Day Holy?

Outside of church attendance, finding data on keeping the Sabbath Day holy can be a somewhat difficult task. Fortunately, a recent study sponsored by the *Deseret News* in Utah provided a wealth of information for us to consider. The 2016 Deseret News Sabbath Day Observance Survey used a nationally representative sample of 1,000 Americans to determine the current state of Sabbath observance in the United States. The results reveal that a majority of Americans (62%) agree it is "important for society to have a day of the week set aside for spiritual rest," and over half (54%) even agree that "public and private organizations should try to accommodate individuals who want to observe a day of rest according to their personal religious traditions, even when it is inconvenient for the organization to do so." But when it came to the Sabbath having "particular religious or spiritual meaning" for the respondents themselves, only 50% reported that it did, down from 74% in a 1978 Gallup poll.[107]

Using the 2016 General Social Survey, Figure 4.1 examines the frequency of church attendance of Americans over time. This is perhaps the most commonly used and one of the most accepted measures of Sabbath Day observance. The clear trend overall is one of declining attendance. In 1980, 36% of respondents reported attending church nearly every week or more, and in 2016, the number was down to just over 29%. While this decrease of 7% is significant, the real story relates to the increase in the percentage who never attend religious services. The mere 12% of individuals who entirely avoided attending church in 1980 more than doubled to 25% in 2016.

---

[107] Monson, Quin and Scott Riding. 2016. *Sabbath Day Observance in the U.S.* Retrieved on December 19, 2017 (https://www.deseretnews.com/media/misc/pdf/DNN-Ten-Today-Sabbath.pdf).

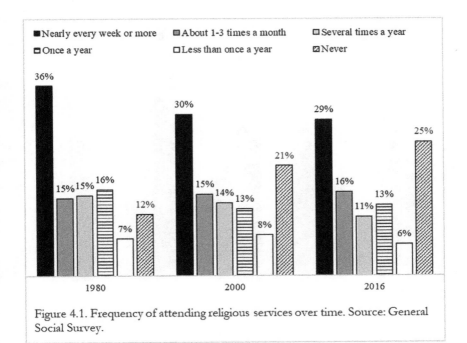

Figure 4.1. Frequency of attending religious services over time. Source: General Social Survey.

When we consider the generational effects, we see that the youngest Americans surveyed are least likely to attend religious services nearly weekly or more and are most likely to never attend. It was found that 22% of the eighteen- to twenty-nine-year-olds attend nearly every week or more while almost twice as many of the sixty-year-olds and older attend that frequently (40%). Inversely, 31% of the youngest respondents never attend church services while 22% of the oldest generation refuse to attend. In both cases, the stated trend moves gradually as age increases (see Figure 4.2).

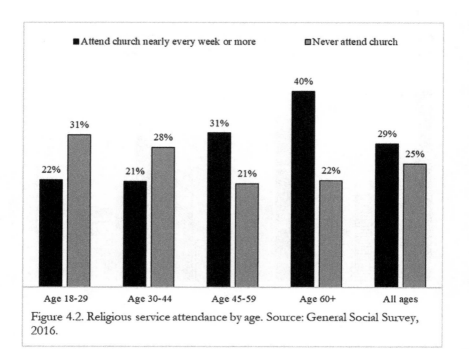

Figure 4.2. Religious service attendance by age. Source: General Social Survey, 2016.

The 2016 Deseret News Sabbath Day Observance Survey asked a series of questions to find out what Americans "usually do on a typical" Sabbath Day. In order to account for variability in religious traditions, respondents were asked each question with the day of the week they personally viewed as the Sabbath inserted. The responses were then compared to similar questions asked on a 1978 Gallup Poll. As figures 4.3 and 4.4 show, there are some noteworthy changes in the way people approach Sabbath Day observance. Of course, their analysis found that significantly fewer people reported attending church, which supports our prior discussion. In contrast, more individuals say they rest and relax on the Sabbath, up to 73% in 2016 from 63% in 1978. While 57% visited friends, neighbors, and relatives on a typically Sabbath in 1978, that number was down to 40% in 2016. About the same percentage, a majority, work around the house on their Sabbath Day (see Figure 4.3).

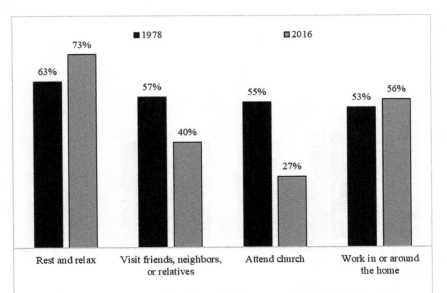

Figure 4.3. Activities respondents "usually do on a typical" Sabbath Day by year. Sources: Deseret News Sabbath Day Observance Survey, 2016. Gallup Poll, 1978.

The percentage who work at a job and pray outside of church have remained fairly stable between the time periods. Shopping, on the other hand, has become a much more common Sabbath Day activity, with 19% of Americans saying it was something they usually do in 1978 rising to 30% in 2016. Fewer people read their religious texts on the Sabbath in 2016 (13%) compared to 1978 (19%). We have also seen a decline in Sabbath Day participation in sports or outdoor activities from 23% in 1978 to 17% in 2016. Finally, as also indicated in Figure 4.4, considerably fewer respondents reported doing religious meditation in 2016 (11% vs. 19%).

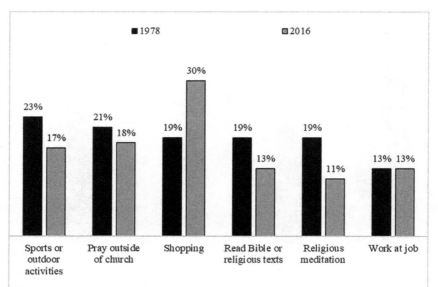

Figure 4.4. Activities respondents "usually do on a typical" Sabbath Day by year. Sources: Deseret News Sabbath Day Observance Survey, 2016. Gallup Poll, 1978.

Jewish Americans have some unique Sabbath Day observances that were captured by a Pew Research survey conducted in 2013 that we also thought would be interesting to include here. They found that 23% of Jews typically light Sabbath candles while only 13% opt not to handle money on the Sabbath.[108] Another Pew report found that a minority of Christians surveyed in 2014 (18%) believed that "resting on the Sabbath" is "essential to what being a Christian means to them" while twice as many (35%) thought attending religious services was essential.[109]

[108] Pew Research Center. 2013. *A Portrait of Jewish Americans*. Retrieved on December 19, 2017 (http://www.pewforum.org/2013/10/01/chapter-4-religious-beliefs-and-practices/).

[109] Pew Research Center. 2016. *Religion in Everyday Life*. Retrieved on December 19, 2017 (http://www.pewforum.org/2016/04/12/essentials-of-christian-identi-ty-vary-by-level-of-religiosity-many-nones-say-honesty-vital-to-being-a-moral-person/).

Evidently, how Americans treat the Sabbath Day has seen some significant changes over the past several decades. Of course, all of these measures could be related back to observance of the second commandment in that they provide evidence of how and how much individuals are focusing on their religious goals and ideals on that particular day versus other pursuits. Whether one believes this or other commandments are being observed well may have a lot to do with specific denominational teachings about what keeping the Sabbath day holy means. Hopefully, something in this chapter will provide additional insights into the meaning of this commandment as it might be subjectively interpreted from unique individual perspectives. As you think about what these perspectives may be, we will shift our focus to children and their parents.

COMMANDMENT 5

"Honour thy father and thy mother"

Honor has many nuances in Hebrew that can express parental devotion. The Hebrew *kābôd*, which is usually rendered into English as *honor*, extends the idea of importance and weightiness to that of glory, splendor, or magnificence. This word is associated with God's majesty that appears to people (Ezekiel 1:28; 3:23; 8:4). Its verbal form is often expressed in deference, actions, and feelings that belong to good human relations such as love, obedience, and support.[110]

Indeed ancient cultures were based on the dichotomy of honor and shame. The relationship of Israel to God in the Bible was often expressed metaphorically in filial terms, and the same verbs of *honoring* and *revering* are used in expressing proper human attitudes to both God and parents. An obligation to respect is enjoined only for God and parents, and the offender in either instance is liable to the extreme penalty of death. These parallels point to the supreme importance that the Torah assigns to the integrity of the family for the sake of the stability of society and generational continuity.[111]

---

[110] Mark F. Rooker. *The Ten Commandments: Ethics for the 21st Century* (Nashville: B&H, 2010), 105.

[111] Nahum M. Sarna. *The JPS Torah Commentary: Exodus* (New York: JPS, 1991), 113.

When one considers Cain's deed as a tiller of the ground in Genesis, it is surprising that he murdered his sibling, who had been created by his parents. A father and a mother produce a life, and that life in turn is sustained by what comes from the earth, the fruit of the ground. There is a recognition that these sources of life are interrelated, that a simultaneous regard for each is required in order for the family unit to survive and sometimes even thrive during a long life upon the land.[112]

In Genesis, many parents seem dishonored, endangering the offenders' ability to prosper in the land. Esau's marriage to a foreign woman was unpleasant to his parents (Genesis 26:35). Jacob tricked his feeble old father. Reuben committed incest and was cursed by his father (Genesis 35:22; 49:3–4). Simeon and Levi dishonored their father by deceiving and murdering the clan of Shechem. Joseph tricked his brothers to ask his father to send his youngest son to Egypt. Rachel dishonored her father by stealing his idols and covering up her theft. Cain dishonored his parents by killing their son. Lot's daughters dishonored their father by getting him drunk and raping him. Noah's son dishonored his father by "seeing his nakedness" and then telling his brothers.[113] According to some ancient legends as recounted above, Terach may have been tricked into giving up his idol worship. Indeed, it can be said that the book of Genesis is a collection of stories about children dishonoring parents, resulting in situations that threatened the survival of the family unit. Some commentators have noted that human beings needed a commandment from on high to resolve their intergenerational conflicts."[114]

Laws outside the Decalogue further elaborate on what dishonoring parents meant: Whoever strikes father or mother should be put to death or whoever curses father or mother should be put to death (Exodus 21:15, 17). *Striking* probably involved causing seri-

---

[112] Calum M. Carmichael. *The Ten Commandments* (Oxford: The Ninth Sacks Lecture, 1983), 4.

[113] "Seeing one's nakedness" is a common English euphemism for a person having sex.

[114] Alan M. Dershowitz. *The Genesis of Justice: Ten Stories of Biblical Injustice that Led to the Ten Commandments and Modern Law* (New York: Warner Books, 2000), 249.

ous bodily harm while *cursing* probably entailed asking a god to do harm.[115] By Moses's time, anyone who cursed a parent could be executed (Exodus 21:17; Leviticus 20:9). Later Eli's sons were disobedient to their father as they disregarded their priestly responsibilities. In contrast to Eli's priestly service, his sons claimed they did not know the Lord and were disobedient to him (1 Samuel 2:12, 31). Absalom stole the heart of Israel and invaded his father's harem (2 Samuel 15:16; 16:21–22).[116]

Serious consequences were prescribed for transgressing the Law. Deuteronomy 21:18–21 declared that parents were expected to take their rebellious children to the elders at the town's gate. After they had provided testimony against their child, the leaders stoned the child to death. In addition, all who dishonored their parents were cursed in Israelite society (Deuteronomy 27:16). Children were expected to keep their father's commands and never forsake their mother's teaching (Proverbs 6:20).[117]

However, Proverbs 30:17 makes this warning: "The eye that mocketh at his father, and despiseth to obey his mother, the ravens of the valley shall pick it out, and the young eagles shall eat it." The psalmist alluded to a blessing from keeping this commandment— that you would see your children's children (Psalm 128:6). The reward for honoring one's elders is, naturally enough, surviving to also become an elderly person (Proverbs 4:10).[118] Conversely, Elijah was expected to arrive to turn the hearts of the children to their parents and the parents to their children to avoid the negative consequences of disobedience.

---

[115] Michael Coogan. *The Ten Commandments: A Short History of An Ancient Text* (New Haven: Yale University Press, 2014), 77.

[116] Mark F. Rooker. *The Ten Commandments: Ethics for the 21ˢᵗ Century* (Nashville: B&H, 2010), 113–114.

[117] Dan Lioy *The Decalogue in the Sermon on the Mount* Studies in Biblical Literature 66 (New York: Peter Lang, 2004), 73.

[118] William H. C. Propp *Exodus 19–40 The Anchor Bible* (New York: Doubleday, 2006), 178.

Judaism of Greco-Roman times emphasized the reciprocal obligations that children had to take care of parents in old age. Ben Sira (second century BCE) admonished children to

> Honor your father in word and deed, so that his blessing may attend you. For a father's blessing establishes the houses of his children, but a mother's curses uproot their foundations. Do not glorify yourself by dishonoring your father, for your father's disgrace is no glory to you. For a man's glory arises from honoring his father, and a neglected mother is a reproach to her children. My child, help your father in his old age, and do not grieve him, as long as he lives. If his understanding fails, be considerate, and do not humiliate him, when you are in all your strength. Charity given to a father will not be forgotten, and will build you up a further atonement for your sins. When you are in trouble you will be remembered; like frost in sunshine, your sins will melt away. He who deserts his father is like a blasphemer, and he who angers his mother is cursed by the Lord.[119]

Failure to return favors with parents brought disgrace that was sometimes considered a form of social death.

In the New Testament, Jesus taught the principle of honoring parents through both word and deed. He set a proper example by being subject to his earthly parents (Luke 2:51). Jesus honored his heavenly Father by doing his will and pleasing him (John 8:29, 49).[120] Jesus also honored his mother's wishes in John 2:1–11 by pro-

---

[119] Ben Sira, III, 1–16; Solomon Goldman. *The Ten Commandments* (Chicago: University of Chicago Press, 1956), 178.

[120] See a discussion about how Jesus honors his Father in Thomas Watson *The Ten Commandments*. Grand Rapids, MI: Christian Classics Ethereal Library (First published as a part of A Body of Practical Divinity, 1692), 129.

viding wine through miraculous means, in contrast to the hypocrisy described in the New Testament toward parents of his age.

During his three-year ministry, Jesus often criticized the Pharisees on their improper observation of the Law of Moses. For example, in Matthew 15:3–9 and Mark 7:11, he rebuked them for hypocritically proclaiming that they followed the fifth commandment when they used the concept of *corban* to dedicate property to the temple so they would not be legally required to use it to take care of their parents. According to Mosaic tradition, any item over which *corban* was pronounced had to be dedicated only to the temple (Leviticus 27) until the Jubilee year which occurred once only every fifty years. In contrast to some contemporaries who neglected their parents, the agonized, crucified Jesus is depicted as honoring his mother when he consigned her to the care of one of his disciples with the words "Behold thy mother!" (John 19:27 KJV).

The apostle Paul discussed the principle of honoring parents as he wrote to Christians who lived throughout the first-century Mediterranean world. He counseled that disobedience to parents leads to evil (Romans 1:30, 2 Timothy 3:2). Furthermore, he admonished the Colossians: "Children, obey your parents in everything, for this pleases the Lord" (Colossians 3:20 NIV). Paul also wrote, "Honor your father and mother—which is the first commandment with a promise—so that it may go well with you and that you may enjoy long life on the earth" (Ephesians 6: 2–3 NIV). In 2 Timothy, disobedience to parents is listed as one of the many signs of living in the last times (2 Tim. 3:1–2). During the medieval period, the Decalogue was interpreted more symbolically to include priests as "fathers" and entailed respecting secular and ecclesiastical hierarchies.[121] Later reformers often encouraged their congregations to honor their parents.

---

[121] John H. Arnold. *Belief and Unbelief in Medieval Europe* (NY: Hodder Arnold, 2005), 36.

Summary

This commandment may have been retroactively given to remedy problems and heartache described in the very early Judeo-Christian tradition. Under the Mosaic Law, punishment was harsh for those who rebelled against their parents, but by the Roman period, writers emphasized reciprocal obligations that grown children needed to fulfill toward their parents. In the New Testament, Jesus fulfilled these obligations, and Paul encouraged others do the same.

How Committed Are Americans to Honoring Their Fathers and Mothers?

Measures related to honoring parents can range anywhere from children taking care of them in their old age to murdering them. Fortunately, children only rarely murder their parents. In fact, in 2010, 242 parents were killed by their offspring (typically adult children), 107 mothers and 135 fathers, accounting for under 2% of all murders.[122] While this might be considered the ultimate act of dishonoring a parent, there are others. The 2012 Measuring Morality Study collected data from 1,519 randomly selected individuals in the United States to explore moral differences in the daily lives of members of the population. At one point in the survey, participants were asked if they would ever curse their parents to their face for money. They were informed that they could apologize for the cursing and explain the situation one year later. Their possible responses included that they would "do it for free" or for $10, $100, $1,000, $10,000, $100,000, $1 million dollars or more, or "never for any amount of money."[123]

---

[122] CBS News. 2012. "Q&A: Why Kids Kill Parents." Retrieved December 22, 2017 (https://www.cbsnews.com/news/qa-why-kids-kill-parents/).

[123] Vaisey, Stephen. 2012. Measuring Morality Study. The data were downloaded from the Association of Religion Data Archives, www.TheARDA.com, and were collected by Stephen Vaisey.

In all, the vast majority of adults (over 79%) said that no amount of money would be enough for them to curse their parents. However, the younger the respondents, the more likely they were to say they would do it for a price. Indeed, 37% of eighteen- to twenty-nine-year-olds claimed they would curse their parents for free or for money while 31% of thirty- to forty-four-year-olds, 13% of forty-five to fifty-nine-year-olds, and only 6% of people over sixty said the same. While most people would never do it, there are some significant generational differences when it comes to willingness to curse one's parents.[124] Interestingly, when Pew Research Center asked respondents in 2014 whether they believed it to be the responsibility of an adult child to provide financial assistance to an aging parent in need, this generational trend was reversed. A total of 86% of eighteen- to twenty-nine-year-olds said adult children *are* responsible and the number gradually declined to 64% of the sixty-five and older respondents agreeing. Overall, 76% of Americans agreed an adult child is responsible to provide such assistance.[125]

When, in the same Pew study, parents sixty-five and older were asked if their adult children had actually helped them in the past twelve months, the majority had not received help. Indeed, 45% reported receiving help with errands, housework, or home repairs, while 12% were helped financially, and only 4% were assisted with personal care such as getting dressed or bathing. When isolating study participants who have parents over the age of 65, 58% claim they helped them with errands, home repairs, or housework in the past month while 28% gave financial help and 14% spent time providing personal care. Of course, these particular numbers do not account for whether parents actually needed help and whether they

---

[124] Vaisey, Stephen. 2012. Measuring Morality Study. The data were downloaded from the Association of Religion Data Archives, www.TheARDA.com, and were collected by Stephen Vaisey.

[125] Parker, Kim and Juliana Menasce Horowitz. 2015. "Family Support in Graying Societies." Pew Research Center. Retrieved December 15, 2017 (http://www. pewsocialtrends.org/2015/05/21/family-support-in-graying-societies/).

received it or not at that point. All in all, when elderly parents in America do get help, 79% of the time it comes from family.[126]

Unfortunately, social scientists typically do not ask adults questions about the quality of relationships with their parents. Consequently, the majority of the evidence related to the more intimate connections children feel toward their parents will come from a survey of youth. The National Study of Youth and Religion (NSYR) conducted in 2003, collected data from 3,370 teenagers (ages thirteen to seventeen). Teens themselves were asked many questions about their relationship with their parents. As Figure 5.1 shows, more than three quarters of teens reported feeling "extremely" or "very" close to their mothers while only 58% felt the same about their fathers. Youth were likewise more likely to say they get along very well with their mothers (69%) compared to their fathers (61%), but the gap was considerably narrower. When it comes to communicating with their parents, more than half of the teenagers (54%) talked at least fairly often to their mother about personal subjects while considerably fewer (31%) spoke with their fathers as often. Only a third of youth felt they have religious beliefs "very similar" to their mothers' or fathers' views.

---

[126] Parker, Kim and Juliana Menasce Horowitz. 2015. "Family Support in Graying Societies." Pew Research Center. Retrieved December 15, 2017 (http://www.pewsocialtrends.org/2015/05/21/family-support-in-graying-societies/).

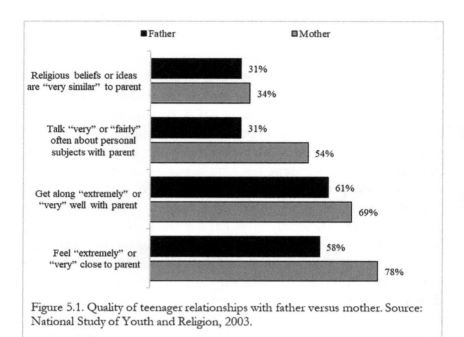

Figure 5.1. Quality of teenager relationships with father versus mother. Source: National Study of Youth and Religion, 2003.

Interestingly, the parents of teenagers who participated in the NSYR were asked to consider how rebellious their teen was in the last year. 32% of parents reported a teen was "somewhat" rebellious or worse. When teens were asked about potentially rebellious behaviors, about one in six reported they did nothing in the last year they hoped their parents would not find out about, and a similar proportion claimed to never have lied to their parents in the last year. Inversely speaking, the vast majority of teens wanted to cover up something and lied to their parents in the preceding year. Only about half, however, felt they had conflicts with their parents over dating choices (see Figure 5.2).

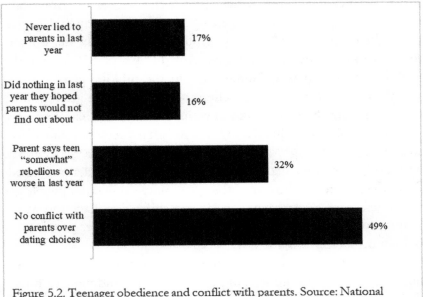

Figure 5.2. Teenager obedience and conflict with parents. Source: National Study of Youth and Religion, 2003.

Outside of parent-child relations, another underlying aspect of this commandment applies to how well society takes care of the elderly more generally. The Bureau of Labor Statistics regularly collects data related to voluntary (unpaid) eldercare in the United States. Their data show that 16% of Americans over the age of 15 provide such care. The majority of the 41.3 million eldercare providers in 2015–2016 (58%) provided care to a parent or grandparent (as opposed to caring for a non-family member) and spent an average of just under three hours a day providing the service.[127]

It is also relevant to examine attitudes about the elderly. The World Values Survey in 2011 collected data from 2, 232 randomly selected individuals and included several questions about their attitudes toward older people (see Figure 5.3). Once again, there are

---

[127] Bureau of Labor Statistics. 2017. "Unpaid Eldercare in the United States—2015–2016 Summary." Retrieved December 19, 2017 (https://www. bls.gov/news.release/elcare.nr0.htm).

some significant age disparities. Just over 68% of all Americans believe older people are not getting respect these days. However, the eighteen to twenty-nine age group is significantly more likely to think so than the sixty and older crowd (74% vs. 61%), with the middle-aged group being somewhere in the middle. People under thirty are also more likely to believe older people are getting more than their fair share from the government (41%), that they have too much political influence (33%), and that they are a burden to society (23%), though only a minority of them agree. In contrast, all those proportions decline among the older respondents. Indeed, fewer than a sixth of those over the age of sixty think older people get too much from government, one in ten think they have too much political influence, and only one in fourteen think older people are a burden on society (Figure 5.3).

Certainly, there are some interesting points to ponder about how well Americans are keeping the fifth commandment to honor their parents. Are enough people respecting, helping, and serving their parents to confidently say the country is generally compliant with this commandment? You must decide. Now that we have had a few chapters to contemplate the "thou shalt" commandments, let us return to a discussion of those things which are forbidden.

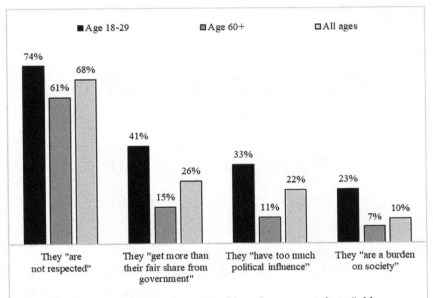

Figure 5.3. Percentage by age who agree with each statement about "older people." Source: World Values Survey, 2011.

COMMANDMENT 6

"Thou shalt not kill"

The commandment against murder is derived from the principle that man is made in God's image (Genesis 1:27) and therefore all human life is considered sacred. God breathed the breath of life into man through his nostrils in the creation narrative (Genesis 2:7). Therefore, life belonged to God alone. God's covenant community was expected to act on God's behalf to take the life of someone who shed the blood of a human being to promote justice.[128] Furthermore, capital punishment was decreed for "whoever sheds the blood of a human being will that person's blood be shed" (Genesis 9:6). The book of Genesis relates the stories of several murderers and attempted murderers including Cain, Lamech, and Levi. Yet none of these individuals were punished by death, so a formal commandment was needed.[129]

The Hebrew *r-ts-h* expressed in this commandment refers to illegal killing, and it is never employed when the subject of the action is God or an angel. This command, when understood in its ancient context, cannot be used to justify either pacifism or the abolition of

---

[128] Walter Harrelson. *The Ten Commandments and Human Rights* (Philadelphia: Fortress, 1980). 110.

[129] See a discussion in Alan M. Dershowitz's *The Genesis of Justice: Ten Stories of Biblical Injustice that Led to the Ten Commandments and Modern Law* (New York: Warner Books, 2000), 249–250.

the death penalty, both of which would have to be argued on other grounds.[130] Under the Mosaic law,

> "If someone strikes another with an iron implement so that he dies, he is a murderer; the murderer should be put to death. Or if someone with a stone in his hand that could cause death strikes another so that he dies, he is a murderer; the murderer should be put to death. Or if someone with a wooden implement in his hand that could cause death strikes another so that he dies, he is a murderer; the murderer should be put to death. (Numbers 35:16–18; compare Deuteronomy 19:11–13) Other biblical laws clarify issues of intentionality: if a homicide is accidental, and that is proven, then the killer is granted asylum; see Numbers 35:22–28 and Deuteronomy 19:4–10. So the commandment's original sense prohibits murder but not other ways of causing death."[131]

Numbers 35:11 makes it clear the Lord was very concerned about unpremeditated, accidental killings. *Ratsach* "applies equally to both cases of premeditated murder and killings as a result of any other circumstances." The latter is "what English Common Law has called, 'manslaughter'". The sixth commandment is based on the biblical concept of the "sanctity of human life." In other words, all human life has intrinsic value and worth, for it is precious in the sight of God (cf. Genesis 1:26–28, 5:1, 9:6, Matthew 5:21–26; James 3:9). This implies that every human life belongs to the Lord, and he alone has the right to take it or command when it should be taken. The sanctity of life derived as a value from this commandment also

---

[130] Nahum M. Sarna. *The JPS Torah Commentary: Exodus* (New York: JPS, 1991), 113.

[131] Michael Coogan. *The Ten Commandments: A Short History of An Ancient Text* (New Haven: Yale University Press, 2014), 81.

means that each individual has divinely sanctioned, inviolable rights and responsibilities to maintain and preserve life (cf. Genesis 9:6–7, Rom. 13:1–7). There was a curse proscribed for whoever secretly murdered his neighbor, and whoever killed—whoever secretly murdered—was doubly cursed (Deut. 27:24) by command of the Lord. Even kings were not exempt from God's punishment. Although David had committed adultery and arranged for the death of Uriah, God knew and announced David's sin through his servant Nathan (2 Samuel 8). Later in the Hebrew Bible, there would be consequences because the Lord made an "inquisition for blood" (Psalm 9:12). David exclaimed, "Deliver me from blood guiltiness, O God" (Psalm 51:14 KJV) in order receive pardon. Some have argued that because of his remorse, this pardon was eventually obtained.

Suicide only rarely occurred in the Hebrew biblical text, and it was depicted in a completely negative light. Saul, who had been cursed through the words of God's prophets and was defeated in battle, fell upon his own sword and killed himself. His armor carrier sadly followed Saul's example (1 Samuel 31:1–5), which became a low-point in the Israelite wars against the Philistines. Prideful Ahithophel could not bear to have his self-perceived wise counsel rejected so "he put his household in order, and hanged himself" (2 Samuel 17:23 KJV). By New Testament times, suicide was a common practice among Gentiles related to preserving honor. In order to discredit him because they thought he had a devil (John 8:52), some of Jesus's critics, according to John's description, wondered if Jesus would commit suicide and thus go away (John 8:22). However, this accusation is contrasted by Jesus's message that if someone keeps his sayings he or she "will not taste of death" (John 8:52). Luke characterizes Jesus's apostle Paul as preventing a jail keeper from taking his own life (Acts 16:28). Sadly, Judas Iscariot committed suicide because of his guilt although the details vary according to Luke and other gospel writers.

There are several New Testament passages that prohibit murder and are founded on this commandment. In Matthew 5:21–24, Jesus declared that the presence of anger and hate against others reveals a murderous disposition and would be in violation of the spirit of the sixth commandment. In the much later times of the Protestant Reformation, the Puritan preacher Thomas Watson argued that ministers are spiritual murderers if they either starve or poison or infect souls.[132]

Originally, however, murder as described in the sixth commandment, occurs when death is inflicted on a *personal* enemy. It did not apply to those executed for violation of the law (Numbers 35:30) nor to the killing of an enemy combatant in battle. This commandment narrowly and specifically prohibited the socially deviant killing of one's personal enemies.[133] Because life belongs to God, if Yahweh were to command his people to commit an act of warfare, then they should feel no compunction in carrying out that kind of action, even though it may result in the death of many.[134]

However, over time the prohibition against murder in the Christian tradition has come to include additional moral principles regarding life and death. Jesus taught in the Sermon on the Mount that those who were angry were already brought to face judgment (Matthew 5:22). Jesus suggested that if one could bridle one's anger, one would never even get close to murder. As Christianity began to spread widely in the fourth-century CE and became a legal religion, the emperor Constantine decided, specifically because of this commandment, to change the longstanding tradition of sentencing convicted criminals to fight as gladiators. The earlier Christian tradition had already banned gladiators from church services. Constantine decided instead that the penalty of fighting as a gladiator was to be replaced by that of forced labor in the mines or quarries "so that those

---

[132] Thomas Watson. *The Ten Commandments*. Grand Rapids, MI: Christian Classics Ethereal Library (First published as a part of A Body of Practical Divinity, 1692), 140.

[133] J. J. Stamm with M. E. Andrew. *The Ten Commandments in Recent Research Studies in Biblical Theology* Second Series 2 (Naperville: Alec R. Allenson, Inc., 1967), 99. The only exception is Numbers 35:30 when it designates the killing of one who is guilty because of the law.

[134] Walter Harrelson. *The Ten Commandments and Human Rights* (Philadelphia: Fortress, 1980), 116.

condemned should pay for their crimes without shedding blood." Constantine's Christian successors also observed the same law.[135]

During the Reformation, Martin Luther similarly believed that the sixth commandment prohibits killing by private individuals but does not abrogate that right for governments.[136] The twentieth-century Christian theologian Karl Barth argued that this commandment included murder, capital punishment, war, abortion, euthanasia, forms of birth control, and even suicide. With the phrase "reverence for life," Barth, following the progressive Christian Albert Schweitzer, "showed how a proper respect for life as God's free gift to humankind rules out in principle the taking of human life under any circumstances except those that lie at the very boundary of what is under any possible circumstances permitted to human beings."[137] Today many progressive groups, whose values derive from Enlightenment ideals of the eighteenth century, oppose war, forbid the killing animals, or oppose the death penalty because if individuals should not murder, then soldiers, butchers, and the state should not either. Yet some of these same progressive groups ironically condone euthanasia and abortion. In summary, the sixth commandment has been interpreted by many in modern Christianity or seemingly progressive groups to further their own interests, belief systems, and agendas.

Summary

Because murder became such a perceived and dangerous problem in early human history, it was forbidden. The ancients believed that human life, being made in the image of God, was sacrosanct. Gradually manslaughter, suicide, and other forms of killing were also

---

[135] The Laws of the *Theodosian Code*, IX, 40, 8, and 11 (in 365 and 367) as quoted in Paul Veyne When Our World Become Christian: 312–394. Translated by Janet Lloyd (Cambridge: Polity, 2010).

[136] Mark F. Rooker. *The Ten Commandments: Ethics for the 21ˢᵗ Century* (Nashville: B&H, 2010), 132–133.

[137] Walter Harrelson *The Ten Commandments and Human Rights* (Philadelphia: Fortress, 1980), 109 quotes Karl Barth, *Church Dogmatics* (Edinburgh: T & T Clark, 1957), 2,2: 683–86; 3.4: 47–564.

prohibited, although killing during wartime was generally accepted. Jesus taught his followers to avoid anger and forgive others, which undercut motivation to kill. Modern religious and secular thinkers tend derive some of their values from different interpretations of this commandment.

How Committed Are Americans to Not Killing?

Each year, the Federal Bureau of Investigation (FBI) collects a tremendous amount of crime data from federal, state, county, local, and university law enforcement agencies across the country. The data is compiled into the Uniform Crime Report (UCR) and is made available to everyone.[138] According to the 2016 report, there were 1,248,185 violent crimes (including murder, rape, robbery, and aggravated assault) counted in the United States. This amounts to at least one act of criminal violence every 25.3 seconds. Out of these more than 1.2 million violent crimes, there were 17,250 murders (one every 30.6 minutes) and 803,007 aggravated assaults (one every 39.4 seconds).[139] While it is certain that nobody wants any form of violence to pervade their neighborhoods or collide with their lives, this method of reporting crime statistics tends to sensationalize it and subsequently cause fear. So just how bad is it? How are we doing compared to years past? The answers might be surprising.

Figure 6.1 provides a sense of the long-term trends related to violent crime. While not all violent crime involves killing, we believed it would be interesting to include some data on assault and overall violent crime in order to provide an expanded context to the discussion. During the past sixty years, there has been tremendous variability in the rates of violent crime, including killing and assault.

---

[138] U.S. Department of Justice, Federal Bureau of Investigation. 2016. "2016 Crime in the United States." Retrieved November 10, 2017 (https://ucr.fbi. gov/crime-in-the-u.s/2016/crime-in-the-u.s.-2016/tables/table-1).

[139] U.S. Department of Justice, Federal Bureau of Investigation. 2016. "2016 Crime in the United States." Retrieved November 10, 2017 (https://ucr.fbi. gov/crime-in-the-u.s/2016/crime-in-the-u.s.-2016/resource-pages/figures/ crime-clock).

The overall trend between the 1960s and 1990s was upward. Violent crime rates went from about 161 crimes per 100,000 inhabitants in 1960 to a peak in the 1990s of almost five times that number. Since the nineties, there has been a steady decline to just under 400 violent crimes per 100,000 people in 2016. The rates of aggravated assault follow an almost identical pattern, maxing out well over 400 in the 1990s, then going down over 40% since that time.

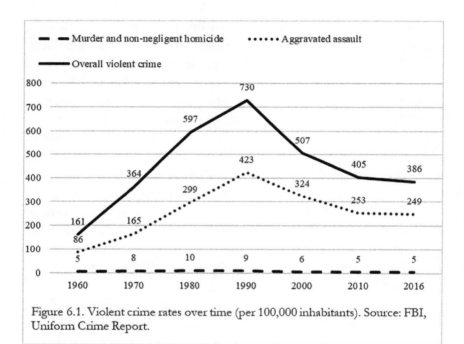

Figure 6.1. Violent crime rates over time (per 100,000 inhabitants). Source: FBI, Uniform Crime Report.

Rates of criminal homicide have followed a somewhat different pattern (see Figure 6.1). The highest rate of the past fifty-six years occurred in 1980, and afterward, the rate remained between about 8 and 10 homicides per 100,000 people into the nineties. Since then, the murder rate has declined sharply, even dropping significantly below 1960 levels. Most recently, however, the homicide rate seems to be moving back upward from a 2014 low of 4.5 occurrences per 100,000 in the population to 4.9 in 2015 and 5.3 in 2016. Whether the new upward trend in killing will continue remains to be seen.

Methods of killing that involve the use of firearms seem to stir significant controversy in modern American society. Even though mass shootings account for a very small percentage of gun-related deaths in the United States, the discussion of gun violence becomes very polarized in light of tragedies like those that occurred in Orlando in 2016, where forty-nine people were killed at the Pulse Nightclub, and Las Vegas in 2017, where fifty-eight people were fatally shot and killed during an outdoor country music concert. Consequently, we thought it would be valuable to examine gun-related deaths. A recent report by the National Center for Health Statistics relates that the rate of gun deaths in the United States rose from about 11 per 100,000 inhabitants in 2015 to about 12 per 100,000 in 2016. It is important to note that only about a third of the recorded gun-deaths were homicides while the other two-thirds were suicides.[140] Overall, firearm homicide deaths have declined sharply in the United States since the peak in the 1990s but have remained fairly steady for the past two decades or so.

Suicide, of course, is not limited by whether or not one has access to a firearm, though about half of all the 42,826 suicides in the United States in 2014 were committed using a gun. Other methods included suffocation, which accounted for 11,407 deaths, and poisoning, which resulted in 6,808 deaths. Overall, the National Center for Health Statistics ranks suicide the tenth most common cause of death in the United States with a yearly rate of over 13 deaths per 100,000 people.[141]

More recent interpretations of the sixth commandment have applied it to controversial issues like abortion and capital punishment. The General Social Survey asked people in the United States whether they "favor or oppose the death penalty for persons convicted of murder." As of 2016, the majority of Americans (61%) still favor using the

---

[140] Ahmad FB, Bastian B. Quarterly provisional estimates for selected indicators of mortality, 2016, Quarter 2, 2017. National Center for Health Statistics. National Vital Statistics System, Vital Statistics Rapid Release Program. 2017.

[141] Kochanek, Kenneth D., Sherry L. Murphy, Jiaquan Xu, and Betzaida Tejada-Vera. 2016. Deaths: Final Data for 2014. National Vital Statistics Reports (65)4. Hyattvill, MD: National Center for Health Statistics.

death penalty for convicted murderers, but overall, there is a downward trend in the percentage of the population that approves. Since 1990, there has been a dramatic drop in the percentage of people who think it is okay to execute convicted criminals (from 79% to 61%).[142] When it comes to actually carry out the death penalty, the United States has been one of the most likely countries to follow through with it over the past decade, ranking seventh internationally behind China, Iran, Saudi Arabia, Iraq, Pakistan, and Egypt.[143] Since 1976, there were 1,465 executions that have been carried out. Between 1976 and 1984, there were only eleven executions carried out, but from that time until 1999, the trend was to increase the number of executions (ranging from 11 to 98 per year). However, from 2000 to the present, the typical inclination has been to execute fewer criminals and only twenty inmates were executed in 2016. As of 2017 there are a total of 2,843 inmates on death row in the United States.[144]

Interestingly, 72% of Republicans support the death penalty while 58% of Democrats and 45% of Independents feel the same way. While the majority of whites (55%) support it, only about a third of racial minorities do, according to a 2016 survey conducted by Pew Research Center.[145] Overall, the Pew data indicates lower levels of favor for the practice than the General Social Survey, but the overall direction of the trends in both surveys are the same.

The trends regarding attitudes about abortion have been a bit more stable. Respondents were asked whether or not they think "it should be possible for a pregnant woman to obtain a legal abortion" under a variety of circumstances (see Figure 6.2). Generally, the minority of

---

[142] Smith, Tom W, Peter Marsden, Michael Hout, and Jibum Kim. General Social Surveys, 1972–2016 [machine-readable data file] /Principal Investigator, Tom W. Smith; Co-Principal Investigator, Peter V. Marsden; Co-Principal Investigator, Michael Hout; Sponsored by National Science Foundation. -NORC ed.- Chicago: NORC at the University of Chicago [producer and distributor].

[143] Masci, David. 2017. "5 Facts about the Death Penalty." Pew Research Center.

[144] Death Penalty Information Center. 2017. "Facts about the Death Penalty". Retrieved November 11, 2017 (https://docs.google.com/viewer?url=https://deathpenaltyinfo.org/documents/FactSheet.pdf).

[145] Masci, David. 2017. "5 Facts about the Death Penalty." Pew Research Center.

Americans think it should possible to get an abortion when there is an out-of-wedlock pregnancy (42%), a woman can't afford (44%), does not want children (46%), or wants an abortion for "any reason" (45%). These numbers have fluctuated slightly since 1980, but overall, most respondents do not approve of abortion under these types of circumstances, and there are no clear trends moving toward greater or lesser acceptance of the practice in these types of situations.

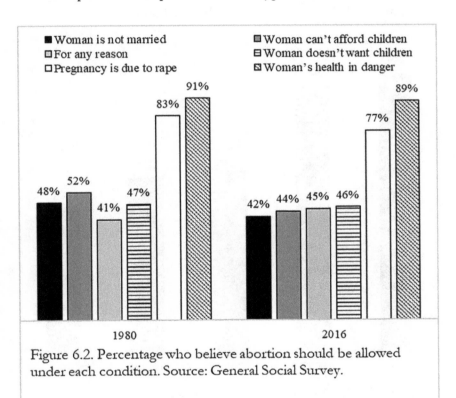

Figure 6.2. Percentage who believe abortion should be allowed under each condition. Source: General Social Survey.

In contrast, when the pregnancy is due to rape or the women's health is in danger, there is widespread support for the idea that abortion should be an option. In 1980, over 83% of those surveyed supported the possibility of abortion in cases of rape, but since then, that number has declined to just over 77%. When the woman's health is in jeopardy, there is overwhelming support for the idea that abortion should be legal. Over the past forty years, around 90% of respondents have been amenable to abortion at such times (see Figure 6.2). What about the actual act of abortion? Since 1970, the total number of legal abortions reported to the Center for Disease Control reached almost 45 million, including 652,639 in 2014, the most recent year for which data is available.[146] Since 1980, the overall ratio of abortions has consistently declined from 359 per 1,000 live births to 186 abortions per 1,000 live births in 2014 (see Figure 6.3).

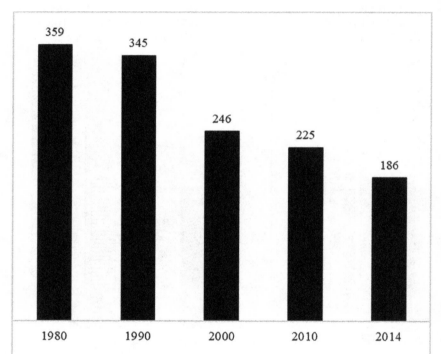

Figure 6.3. Number of legal abortions per 1,000 live births. Source: Centers for Disease Control and Prevention, Abortion Surveillance Report.

---

[146] Centers for Disease Control and Prevention. "Abortion Surveillance Report." Retrieved November 11, 2017 (https://www.cdc.gov/reproductivehealth/data_stats/abortion.htm).

There certainly seem to be some interesting trends and controversies in the United States related to the sixth commandment.
While some types of behaviors related to it seem to be happening
less, some are still regular occurrences in our society. Are we doing
well keeping the commandment not to kill? As you deeply ponder
this, let's turn to the issue of adultery.

COMMANDMENT 7

"Thou shalt not commit adultery"

Marriage and procreation are central societal interests in the Judeo-Christian tradition. This tradition began with Adam and Eve, whom God commanded to be fruitful and multiply and replenish the earth (Genesis 1:27). Then God commanded Adam to "leave his father and his mother, and . . . cleave unto his wife: and they shall be one flesh" (Genesis 2:24) thereby promoting the ideal unity through marriage after God brought them together (Genesis 2:22). It naturally follows that adultery is a poisoning of the natural order of unity. Unity is a principle of creation itself so when a man joins himself to another, he is transgressing against what God commanded when Adam and Eve were created.

Although marriage was a common and almost ordinary theme in many early Near Eastern cultures, procreation was still thought of as a beautiful enigma. Many ancient societies understood themselves to be related to the realm of the gods through procreation. "The bringing of fertility to earth itself came about through the sacred marriage of the gods, one issue of which was such fruitfulness on earth, animal life, some plant life, and the life of human beings in particular were all, in the sharing the process of creation and renewal of life on the earth."[147] Marriage, procreation, and sexuality were associated with the divine in early times.

However, according to Genesis, uncontrolled sexuality caused much grief in early human history. "There were numerous stories of forbidden sex (or at least close calls)—Sarah and Rivka [Rebecca] with the kings; Lot with his daughters; Tamar with her father-in-law; Reuben with his father's mistress [Genesis 35:22]; Potiphar's wife with Joseph—enough to warrant a specific prohibition in the Ten Commandments."[148] Leviticus 20:10 forbade intercourse with unmarried women. Rabbi Abraham Ibn Ezra (CE 1089–1167), perhaps the greatest medieval Jewish scholar, recognized that there were grades in adultery, the gravity of the sin depending on whether the one with whom it is committed was unmarried, in her menstrual period, married, a heathen, male, or beast. The rabbis applied the commandment also to masturbation. But specific references to adultery are limited in the Pentateuch to the two Decalogues and Leviticus 20:10.[149]

There are many nuances to the Hebrew *n'p*, often rendered into English as *adultery*, that define what this commandment means. Adultery (*n'p*) has traditionally been defined as sexual intercourse between a man, married or not, and a married woman who is not his wife. Such was the definition of adultery throughout the ancient Near East. Adultery was a private wrong committed against the husband, an infringement of his exclusive rights of possession.[150] Rabbi Ibn Ezra regarded *n'p* as connoting all forbidden sexual relations.

---

[147] Walter Harrelson. *The Ten Commandments and Human Rights* (Philadelphia: Fortress, 1980), 126.

[148] Alan M. Dershowitz *The Genesis of Justice: Ten Stories of Biblical Injustice that Led to the Ten Commandments and Modern Law* (New York: Warner Books, 2000), 250.

[149] Solomon Goldman *The Ten Commandments* (Chicago: University of Chicago Press, 1956), 183.

[150] Nahum M. Sarna. *The JPS Torah Commentary: Exodus* (New York: JPS, 1991), 114.

Israelite tribal affiliation was transmitted only through fathers; thus, the entire kinship system depended on female marital fidelity.[151]

Over time, however, the significance of the term and the connotations associated with it seemed to deepen and widen. For example, the term was also used to refer to idolatrous worship and unfaithfulness to God. The emphasis of the seventh commandment is on safeguarding "the integrity of the husband-wife relationship" through sexual purity and fidelity. The injunction stands in sharp contrast with the promiscuity and infidelity of many ancient and modern cultures alike. From God's perspective, adultery is a grievous offense against him, people, and society, for it represents a reprehensible breach of the marriage covenant (Malachi 2:14–15).

Adultery also signifies a willful violation of the divine ideal (Genesis 2:24). His intent for marriage was that man and the woman should be committed to each other for life and share in the creative work of making new people (Genesis 2:23)."[152] Through his transgression, an adulterer revealed his lack of judgment (Hosea 4:11–14) and not only destroyed his own reputation but also opened himself up to unexpected trials and hardships (Proverbs 6:32–35). These adulterers who soiled their neighbor's wife also defiled themselves with the illicit partner (Leviticus 18:20). This crime was so serious that the Israelite community was to execute the transgressors (20:10), either by stoning or by strangulation. In this way, the evil would be purged from Israel (Deuteronomy 22:22).[153]

In an honor/shame culture, through purging this evil, a male would no longer be "dishonoring a male of one's community by having sexual relations with his wife. The dishonor consists in the adulterer's ability to cross another's family boundaries with impunity. As a dishonor to family reputation, adultery requires satisfaction that can often lead to interminable wrangling, potential blood feuds, and

---

[151] William H. C. Propp. *Exodus 19–40 The Anchor Bible* (New York: Doubleday, 2006), 179.

[152] Dan Lioy. *The Decalogue in the Sermon on the Mount* Studies in Biblical Literature 66 (New York: Peter Lang, 2004), 75.

[153] Dan Lioy. *The Decalogue in the Sermon on the Mount* Studies in Biblical Literature 66 (New York: Peter Lang, 2004), 76.

death for individuals and occasionally for even whole communities. To prevent this, Israelite law required both individuals caught in adultery to be killed (Deuteronomy 22:22)."[154]

Adultery had many negative consequences for individual men and women and, most importantly, weakened the social glue which held together Israelite society, so harsh measures were instituted as a deterrent. One proverb counsels, "Do not desire her beauty in your heart, and do not let her capture you with her eyelashes; for the price of a prostitute is only a loaf of bread, but (the adulteress) hunts down a precious life" (Proverbs 6:25–26). Another proverb counsels, "Can a man carry fire next to his chest and his clothes not be burned?" (Proverbs 6:27). Lust leads men and women into shame and disgrace (Proverbs 6:32-33).[155] Job's remedy was this:

> "I made a covenant with my eyes not to look lustfully at a girl" (Job 31:1 NIV). Much later in the Jewish tradition, Philo wrote that adultery made "havoc of three families: of that of the husband who suffers from the breach of faith, stripped of the promise of the marriage-vows and his hopes of legitimate offspring, and of two others, those of the adulterer and the woman, for the infection of the outrage and dishonor and disgrace of the deepest kind extends to the family of both."[156]

---

[154] Bruce J. Malina and Richard L. Rohrbaugh. *Social-Science Commentary on the Synoptic Gospels* 2nd Edition (Minneapolis: Fortress Press, 2003), 45.

[155] Philip Graham Ryken. *Written in Stone: The Ten Commandments and Today's Moral Crisis* (Phillipsburg, NJ: P&R Publishing, 2010), 159.

[156] Philo. *Decalogue* 126-131: Philo continues about adultery: "And if their connections include a large number of persons through intermarriages and widespread associations, the wrong will travel all round and affect the whole State. Very painful, too is the uncertain status of the children, for if the wife is not chaste there will be doubt and dispute as to the real paternity of the offspring. Then if the fact is undetected, the fruit of the adultery usurp the position of the legitimate and form an alien and bastard brood and will ultimately succeed to the heritage of their putative father to which they have no right. And the

In the New Testament, sexuality became even more regulated for Christians. Jesus taught that one should avoid lustful thoughts that were the equivalent to adultery (Matthew 5:28). Only if divorce was absolutely necessary because of fornication could a man abandon his wife. If he divorced her for other reasons, she and her future spouse would become adulterers (Matthew 5:32). Jesus also called out a Samaritan woman at the well for having been married five times and living in an adulterous relationship (John 4) while at the same time encouraging her to accept him as the Messiah. He offered the "living water" of his message to her and her town—and they subsequently accepted it. Throughout the New Testament (for example, in John's Revelation 3:12; 21:2, 9–10; 22:17), marriage between Christ and the church (symbolized by a bride) is a theme that indirectly but subtly emphasizes the sanctity of marriage, especially when abruptly contrasted by the fornication associated with Babylon.

Jesus's apostles often admonished Christians in their epistles to avoid fornication. Fornication, which renders the Greek *porneia*, included a very wide range of inappropriate sexual activity, including prostitution. The apostle Peter warned his readers against having "eyes full of adultery" (2 Peter 2:14). Paul counseled married Corinthians to "not deprive each other" of sexual relations (1 Corinthians 7:3, 5) which prevented lust and potential adultery. Paul warned, "Do you not know that the unrighteous will not inherit the kingdom of God? Do not be deceived: neither the sexually immoral, nor idolaters, nor adulterers, nor men who practice homosexuality . . . will inherit the kingdom of God" (1 Corinthians 6:9–10).

---

adulterer having in insolent triumph vented his passions and sown the seed of shame, his lust now sated, will leave the scene and go on the way mocking at the ignorance of the victim of his crime, who like a blind man knowing nothing of the covert intrigues of the past will be forced to cherish the children of his deadliest foe as his own flesh and blood. On the other hand, if the wrong becomes known, the poor children who have done no wrong will be most unfortunate, unable to be classed with either family, either the husband's or the adulterer's. Such being the disasters wrought by illicit intercourse, naturally the abominable and God-detested sin of adultery was placed first in the list of wrongdoing."

The epistle to the Hebrews reads, "Let marriage be held in honor by all, and let the marriage bed be undefiled, for God will judge the sexually immoral and adulterous" (Hebrews 13:4). Paul's epistle to the Romans even specifically addressed homosexuality: "Even their women exchanged natural sexual relations for unnatural ones. In the same way, the men also abandoned natural relations with women and were inflamed with lust for one another. Men committed shameful acts with other men, and received in themselves the due penalty for their error" (Romans 1:26–27 NIV). Paul considered sexual relations with a prostitute an abominable substitute for marriage (1 Corinthians 6:15–20). He chided the Corinthians for gross immorality because (1 Corinthians 5:1 NASB) "it is actually reported that there is immorality among you, and immorality of such a kind as does not exist even among the Gentiles, that someone has his father's wife."

According to Luke, James spoke, "But that we write unto them, that they abstain from pollutions of idols, and from *fornication* (*porneia*), and from things strangled, and from blood" (Acts 15:20 KJV). Paul considered practices like circumcision as theologically unnecessary in his writings (Galatians 5), but he still emphasized the significance of the seventh commandment in Gentile Christian circles. The author of Hebrews wrote that "whoremongers and adulterers God will judge" (Hebrews 13:4 KJV). Peter admonished, "The Lord knoweth how to reserve the unjust to the day of judgement to be punished, but chiefly them that walk in the lust of uncleanness" (2 Peter 2:9 KJV). The New Testament is notably saturated with writing promoting covenantal monogamy in a tradition of limited sexuality. In later centuries of the medieval period, celibacy was promoted, based on an interpretation of 1 Corinthians 7 as the highest ideal, thereby completely prohibiting sexuality.[157] For those who could not live according this lofty ideal, Augustine taught married

---

[157] For a good discussion on this topic over first six centuries of Christian history, see Henry Chadwick *The Church in Ancient Society: From Galilee to Gregory the Great* (Oxford: Oxford University Press, 2003).

people that adultery destroys trust and fidelity, and therefore destroys one's humanity (*c. Jul.* 2.4).[158]

During the Reformation, long-held attitudes about celibacy began to change. Although he eventually rejected celibacy through marrying a former nun, Martin Luther wrote in the tradition of limited sexuality of the Reformation, "This commandment applies to every form of unchastity however it is called. Not only is the external act forbidden, but also every kind of cause, motive, and means. Your heart, your lips, and your whole body are to be chaste and to afford no occasion, aid, or encouragement to unchastity."[159]

The Westminster Shorter Catechism simply stated: "The Seventh Commandment requireth the preservation of our own and our neighbor's chastity, in heart, speech, and behavior."[160] During the Reformation and Counter-Reformation of the sixteenth century, there was an attempt to introduce the death penalty of the Old Testament into secular law for adultery. Pope Sixtus V, a zealous reformer, authorized the death penalty for adultery in Rome in 1586. "However, more commonly Reformed Protestantism, with its emphasis on the positive value of Old Testament law, was the setting for such legal innovations. Calvin's Geneva led the way and Scotland was not far behind—in both cases, the admittedly small number of those who were executed were persistent offenders."[161]

In all such legislation there was a double standard which demanded harsher penalties for an adulterous married woman than for adulterous married men who were punished as mere fornicators with fines or only detention.[162] Today this commandment is some-

---

[158] Henry Chadwick *The Church in Ancient Society: From Galilee to Gregory the Great* (Oxford: Oxford University Press, 2003), 396.

[159] Martin Luther. *The Large Catechism,* trans. Robert H. Fischer (Philadelphia: Fortress, 1959), 36 quoted in Philip Graham Ryken *Written in Stone: The Ten Commandments and Today's Moral Crisis* (Phillipsburg, NJ: P&R Publishing, 2010), 158.

[160] (A. 71) quoted in Philip Graham Ryken *Written in Stone: The Ten Commandments and Today's Moral Crisis* (Phillipsburg, NJ: P&R Publishing, 2010), 158.

[161] Diarmaid MacCulloch *The Reformation* (New York: Penguin, 2005), 635–636.

[162] Diarmaid MacCulloch *The Reformation* (New York: Penguin, 2005), 635–636.

times interpreted as a sweeping statement about sexual morality. The Catechism of the Catholic Church includes as "offenses" against this commandment masturbation, fornication, pornography, prostitution, rape, homosexuality, contraception, and artificial insemination, as well as divorce, polygamy, incest, and, of course, adultery.[163]

Summary

Procreation is ordained of God in Genesis to promote happiness and unity. Limiting sexuality to marriage was prescribed to remedy many of the problems that occurred in Genesis. Strict laws associated with Moses prohibiting specific sexual sins were enforced with punishments up to death. Sexuality was limited—only within the bond of matrimony, including polygamy, and was a defining article of the Law of Moses. Unlike much of the Mosaic Law that was eventually jettisoned as it was transcended by Christianity, any form of fornication, adultery, homosexual relations, or even lustful thoughts and especially actions were forbidden by both Jesus and his apostles. While marriage was still considered honorable, some later Christian leaders often promoted celibacy as the highest ideal while others in the Protestant tradition considered marriage perfectly respectable.

How Committed Are Americans to Not Committing Adultery?

A casual glance at American media reveals a significant sexualization of popular culture. Television, movies, magazines, websites, and books are fraught with depictions of nudity and sexual activity. But what of American sexual attitudes and behaviors? There are a lot of ways to approach a discussion about adherence to the seventh commandment. When it comes to attitudes and behaviors related to sexuality, there are many that we could examine; indeed this is a topic

---

[163] http://www.scborromeo.org/ccc/p3s2c2a6.htm. Michael Coogan *The Ten Commandments: A Short History of An Ancient Text* (New Haven: Yale University Press, 2014), 83.

about which a lot of data has been collected. We decided to draw primarily from what is available in the 2016 General Social Survey,[164] so we can be confident that the numbers we present closely reflect what is happening in the United States nationwide.

Most of the data about attitudes involved asking individuals if they believed various behaviors were "always wrong," "almost always wrong," "sometimes wrong," or "not wrong at all." Of course, the commandment against adultery does not include an "unless" or an "except," so we could accomplish our purposes by focusing solely on the "always wrong" category. However, because it is intriguing to examine extremes and to give a clearer idea of what is happening, we will discuss the percentages falling into the "not wrong at all" group as well.

Adult survey respondents were asked if they felt it was wrong to "have sex before marriage." The majority of Americans (about 60%) believe it is not wrong at all to engage in premarital sex while only 20% believe it is always wrong (Figure 7.1). Younger people ages eighteen to twenty-nine (16%) are much less likely than those over 60 (28%) to think it is always wrong to have sex before marriage (Figure 7.2).

The National Study of Youth and Religion conducted in 2003 asked over 3,300 teenagers a similar question and found about 60% of them responded that people should wait to have sex until they are married.[165] When asked what they actually do, 21% of all teenagers reported having sexual intercourse at least once, but this varied significantly by age. More than 97% of the youngest teenagers

---

[164] Smith, Tom W, Peter Marsden, Michael Hout, and Jibum Kim. General Social Surveys, 1972-2016 [machine-readable data file] /Principal Investigator, Tom W. Smith; Co-Principal Investigator, Peter V. Marsden; Co-Principal Investigator, Michael Hout; Sponsored by National Science Foundation. -NORC ed.- Chicago: NORC at the University of Chicago [producer and distributor].

[165] The National Study of Youth and Religion, http://youthandreligion.nd.edu/, whose data were used by permission here, was generously funded by Lilly Endowment Inc., under the direction of Christian Smith, of the Department of Sociology at the University of Notre Dame and Lisa Pearce, of the Department of Sociology at the University of North Carolina at Chapel Hill.

(thirteen-year-olds) reported never having had sex while only 52% of the seventeen-year-olds had remained abstinent, with almost 30% of the age group stating they had engaged in sexual intercourse "several times" or "many times." With each birthday, the likelihood that teenagers have engaged in premarital sex increases dramatically.

When adults were asked about whether or not children in their early teens (ages fourteen to sixteen) should have sex before marriage, nearly 62% of respondents deemed it always wrong while just under 10% thought it to be perfectly okay (Figure 7.1). Again, as shown on Figure 7.2, fewer of the youngest people (50%) seem to absolutely oppose the idea than the oldest (71%). Clearly, the age of the individual who might engage in fornication greatly influences people's attitudes about whether or not it is morally wrong. Indeed, people are three times more likely to denounce premarital sex for early teens than will do so for all who have yet to marry.

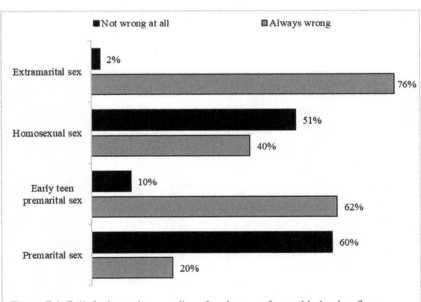

Figure 7.1. Beliefs about the morality of each type of sexual behavior. Source: General Social Survey, 2016.

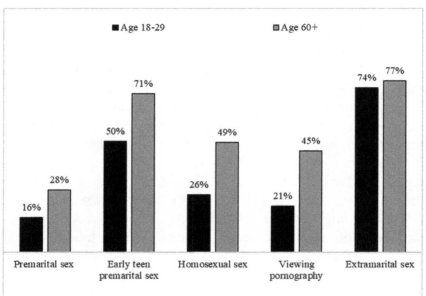

Figure 7.2. Percentage by age who believe each behavior is always wrong. Source: General Social Survey, 2016.

The rightness or wrongness of homosexual sex is another hotly debated topic in American society. While some might consider it less relevant to a discussion of the seventh commandment, historically most issues related to sexuality have been connected to it. Figure 7.1 reveals that attitudes about homosexuality seem to be the most evenly split of all the issues we are considering. In fact, more than half of Americans see nothing wrong with homosexual sex while 4 in 10 believe it is always wrong.

The age gap is very evident here again in Figure 7.2. Only one-fourth of the youngest generation see it as absolutely wrong while nearly half of those over sixty see it as always wrong. A 2013 study of almost 35,000 adults by the Center for Disease Control found that 1.5% of women and 1.8% of men report being lesbian or gay while 0.4% of men and 0.9% of women say they are bisexual, the younger age groups being considerably more likely to identify as gay, lesbian, or bisexual than older age groups.[166]

Pornography consumption is another issue closely tied to sexual morality. A 2008 study of 813 students at six universities in the United States found widespread acceptance and use of pornography. In fact, half of surveyed women and two thirds of men reported finding pornography use acceptable while 87% of men and a third of women reported using pornography themselves.[167] Interestingly, among college-aged men, it appears that thinking pornography is wrong does not prevent one from using it. The authors of the study also found some evidence that exposure to pornography promotes risky sexual behavior.

Society-wide, only 21% of eighteen- to twenty-nine-year-olds compared to nearly half of adults over sixty believe pornography should be "illegal to all" whereas the majority of all adults (69%) would have it unrestricted or only restricted for minors.[168] Finally, when it comes to attitudes about the act of committing adultery itself, it seems the vast majority of Americans (76%) consider it "always wrong" to cheat on a spouse while only 2% view it as "not wrong at all" and the young and old are equally as likely to see it as wrong (see Figures 7.1 and 7.2). This reveals a very strong social norm against the act of adultery.

Attitudes and behaviors surrounding marriage can also be tied to the seventh commandment. In fact, historically, this commandment was connected to an emphasis on the importance of unity within marriage. Consequently, we examined marital status and

---

[166] Ward, Brian W., James M. Dahlhamer, Adena M. Galinsky, and Sarah S. Joestl. 2013. *Sexual Orientation and Health Among U.S. Adults: National Health Interview Survey, 2013.* Center for Disease Control National Health Statistics Report.

[167] Carroll J, Padilla-Walker LM, Nelson LJ. "Generation XXX: Pornography acceptance and use among emerging adults." Journal of Adolescent Research. 2008(23):6–30.

[168] Smith, Tom W, Peter Marsden, Michael Hout, and Jibum Kim. General Social Surveys, 1972–2016 [machine-readable data file] /Principal Investigator, Tom W. Smith; Co-Principal Investigator, Peter V. Marsden; Co-Principal Investigator, Michael Hout; Sponsored by National Science Foundation. -NORC ed.- Chicago: NORC at the University of Chicago [producer and distributor].

marital satisfaction. It might surprise many to discover that at any given time, almost all married people (96%) report being "happy" or "pretty happy" with their marriages. In 2016, only 4% of respondents claimed to be "not too happy" with their marriages (Figure 7.3). At the time of the survey, 14% of respondents reported their current marital status as divorced. When looking at all those who have ever been married, almost 42% report having experienced a divorce or separation. It would seem that despite the fact that the vast majority of people are happy with their marriages at any given time, a high percentage experience periods of separation or get divorced.

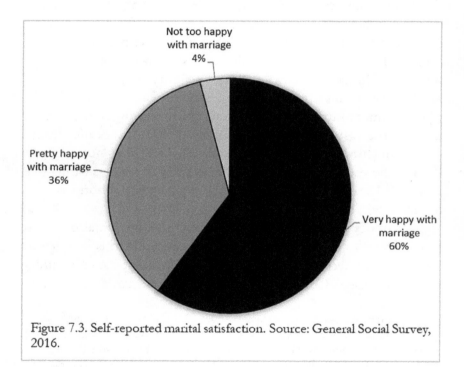

Figure 7.3. Self-reported marital satisfaction. Source: General Social Survey, 2016.

When it comes to sexual attitudes some interesting trends are evident, but what about when considering actual sexual behaviors? It seems clear that there is a portion of the population that holds to attitudes that might be viewed as encouraging of more uninhibited sexual activity. But what are individuals actually doing? Two types of behaviors related to the command to not commit adultery are prostitution and promiscuity. To get a sense of general sexual promiscuity, we examined whether unmarried individuals had two or more sex partners in the last twelve months. While we acknowledge that this is not a perfect measure and that some might find it oversimplified, we believe it is relevant to the question at hand. We found that 24% of singles had two or more sexual partners during the twelve months before they took the survey. About twice as many men (31%) as women (17%) had multiple partners in the previous year. It is probably not surprising to many that men are over five times more likely to have ever paid or been paid for sex than women (11% vs. 2%). In total, about 6% of Americans have paid or been paid for sex.

Now that we have considered various beliefs, behaviors, and attitudes related to keeping the seventh commandment, we turn our focus to the specific act of adultery itself. In the United States, about one in six people (17%) report that they have engaged in extramarital sex at some point in their lives. It is important to keep in mind that because these are self-reports and people tend to shy away from admitting to socially undesirable activities, we can be confident that adultery is even more prevalent than these numbers indicate. Unfortunately, there is no way to know for sure just how much lower the numbers are than they should be (see Figure 7.4).

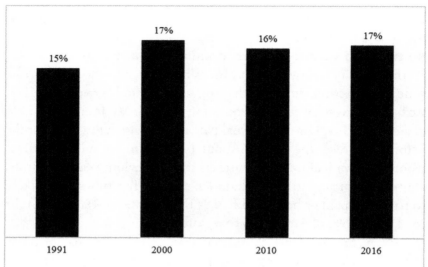

Figure 7.4. Percentage who have ever had extramarital sex over time. Source: General Social Survey.

When examining adultery and attitudes toward it over time, there seems to be quite a bit of stability (Figure 7.4). The proportion of the population that has committed adultery since 1990 is hovering in the 15–17% range. This same pattern holds true for the percentage of individuals who condemn adultery as "always wrong." While there was a strong increase in the number who disapprove of the behavior between 1980 and 1990, for a few decades afterward, the disapproval rate remained around 80%. The data from 2016 indicates a 4% drop compared to 2010 in the number who always oppose cheating. Only time will tell if this decline holds, increases, or whether it is an anomaly. Even so, overall, the trend seems fairly steady.

COMMANDMENT 8

"Thou shalt not steal"

Stealing occurs even in the very beginning of the Judeo-Christian tradition and thoroughly permeates it. Although God commanded, "Of every tree of the Garden thou shalt freely eat," Adam and Eve violated this command by taking fruit from a prohibited tree which some in Christendom have interpreted as theft. Later in Genesis, Rachel's theft of her father Laban's idols brought about conflict between him and her husband Jacob that could have ended tragically.[169] Blind competitiveness and jealousy may have been the essence of the devil's pride when he tried to steal God's honor by exalting his throne (Isaiah 14:12–13; cf. Revelation 12:7–9) and of Cain's pride when he killed Abel (Genesis 4:4–8) and of Rebekah's and Jacob's pride when they seem to have stolen Esau's birthright (Genesis 27).[170]

As the ancient Israelite society adopted norms of equity, stealing became a source of friction. While punishment for stealing was often harsh, capital punishment did not result unless a human being was stolen (Exodus 21:16). Furthermore, only in a just society with some accompanying notion of property rights could prohibitions against

---

[169] Alan M. Dershowitz. *The Genesis of Justice: Ten Stories of Biblical Injustice that Led to the Ten Commandments and Modern Law* (New York: Warner Books, 2000), 250.

[170] J. I. Packer. *The Ten Commandments* (Wheaton: Tyndale House, 1989), 60.

theft exist. The ancient legislation of Israel clarifies that impartial judgment is the ideal: no partiality was to be shown to any person, not to the rich in defiance of the rights of the poor and not to the poor in defiance of the rights of others. A call to impartial judgment is found in Leviticus 19:15.[171] The Israelite covenant community was expected to be fair, especially with the weak and poor because they were oppressed in Egypt.[172]

In time, prohibitions against theft were again emphasized in the Hebrew Bible and sometimes enforced as property rights seem to have become more significant. Achan stole a forbidden wedge of gold, which separated his soul from God (Joshua 7:21). In the Mosaic Law, theft of food was even prohibited: "When thou comest into the standing corn of thy neighbour, thou shalt not move a sickle unto thy neighbour's corn" (Deuteronomy 23:25 KJV). The poor were characterized as needing extra help in the form of interest free loans within the community of God's people (Leviticus 25:35–38, Deuteronomy 15:7–8). Nevertheless, the book of Proverbs warns that laziness leads to poverty (Proverbs 6:10–11), which is one factor which tempts the poor to steal (Proverbs 30:8–9).[173]

In New Testament times, perceived limited material resources often became the source of contention and led to the heightened

---

[171] Walter Harrelson. *The Ten Commandments and Human Rights* (Philadelphia: Fortress, 1980), 139.

[172] Walter Harrelson. *The Ten Commandments and Human Rights* (Philadelphia: Fortress, 1980), 137. Harrison wrote, "The community was required by the covenant law not to deal violently with the weak and the poor and those left without normal supports of family life. They were to remember that they—each individual Israelite—were all descendants of slaves in Egypt, persons oppressed by those more wealthy and powerful than they. They were never to forget this fact. They should know the heart of the oppressed, the stranger, the poor, the victimized; how could they then become victimizers, oppressors, hostile to the stranger in their midst? To do so would be to impose on others the very conditions of life in which their God once found them and from which, out of his mercy, he delivered them."

[173] See a discussion in Philip Graham Ryken *Written in Stone: The Ten Commandments and Today's Moral Crisis* (Phillipsburg, NJ: P&R Publishing, 2010), 173, 176.

sense of anxiety about potential theft that permeated the lower classes. In the ancient Mediterranean, the rich were considered either thieves or the heirs of thieves since all good things in life were viewed as limited, so the only way one could get ahead was to steal from others.[174]

The rich young man was perceived by his contemporaries as being greedy, and this perception was confirmed when he would not give all of his goods to the poor and follow Jesus (Matthew 19:16–22). When Jesus is challenged by critics for breaking the Sabbath and theft, the reader learns that the Mosaic Law as commonly interpreted in this time did not forbid people from picking food and eating while in the field (see Matthew 12:1, Mark 2:23, Luke 6:1). Individuals were forbidden, however, from cutting it and hauling it away for later consumption. Jesus later challenged that the priestly families in charge of the Temple, a source of great wealth, "were rich," a term that, as noted above, could be equally well translated *greedy* and *vicious*. Given a limited good view of the world, if the Jerusalem Temple personnel and their supporters were amassing wealth stored in the "den of thieves" (Matthew 21:13, Luke 19:46), then large numbers of persons were simultaneously becoming poor and unable to maintain their honor as "sons of Israel."[175] Philo also held this ancient Mediterranean view of the rich of New Testament times:

> So all thieves who have acquired the strength rob whole cities, careless of punishment because their high distinction seems to set them above the laws. These are oligarchically-minded persons, ambitious for despotism or domination, who perpetrate thefts on a great scale, disguising the real fact of robbery under the grand-sounding names of government and leadership.[176]

---

[174] Bruce J. Malina and Richard L. Rohrbaugh. *Social-Science Commentary on the Synoptic Gospels* 2nd Edition (Minneapolis: Fortress Press, 2003), 99.

[175] Bruce J. Malina and Richard L. Rohrbaugh. *Social-Science Commentary on the Synoptic Gospels* 2nd Edition (Minneapolis: Fortress Press, 2003), 401.

[176] Philo. *Decalogue* 135–136.

Philo's statement describes many of the elite of the Greco-Roman world who illegally possessed the earth. He, like many later Christians, looked forward to a time when the poor would inherit it instead (Psalm 37:11).

In their writings, Jesus's apostles discourage theft and instead promoted the virtues of industry, thankfulness, and honesty. Paul wrote, "Let him that stole steal no more, but rather let him labour, working with his hands" (Ephesians 4:28 KJV). We read in Hebrews to "be content with such things as ye have" (Hebrews 13:5 KJV). In 1 Timothy 6:6–8 (NIV), Paul advises Timothy that "godliness with contentment is great gain. For we brought nothing into the world, and we can take nothing out of it. But if we have food and clothing, we will be content with that." In James 5:4 (KJV), the rich are strongly admonished to be honest with workers because the "hire of the labourers who have reaped down your fields, which is of you kept by fraud, crieth: and the cries of them which have reaped are entered into the ears of the Lord of Sabaoth."

Certainly, all human beings depend on certain basic, life-sustaining material resources for a balanced and fulfilled life. In the ancient Mediterranean, the rich were often considered as those who had taken more than their fair share and were therefore guilty before God of stealing. Therefore, stealing infringed on the very extensions of oneself, and they threatened community living and unity.

The theme of possessing very limited wealth is also found in the words of the famous fourth-century CE preacher Chrysostom, who said, "I beg you remember this without fail, that not to share our own wealth with the poor is theft from the poor and deprivation of their means of life: we do not possess our own wealth but theirs."[177]

During the Reformation, Protestant figures struggled to define theft through the changing economic conditions of early modern Europe in which resources were no longer thought of as being so

---

[177] John Chrysostom. *On Wealth and Poverty*, trans. Catherine Roth (New York: St. Vladmir's Seminary, 1984), 55.] Philip Graham Ryken *Written in Stone: The Ten Commandments and Today's Moral Crisis* (Phillipsburg, NJ: P&R Publishing, 2010), 177.

limited in a zero-sum game. Calvin wrote, "Let us remember that all those arts whereby we acquire the possessions and money of our neighbors—when such devices depart from sincere affection to a desire to cheat or in some manner to harm—are to be considered as thefts."[178] Martin Luther wrote that the meaning of this commandment is to "take advantage of our neighbor in any sort of dealing that results in loss to him."[179]

Today many view accumulation of wealth, in the spirit of the Protestant work ethic, as a blessing from God—a sign of his good favor. In contrast, many Progressives promote economic equality by focusing the concept of theft of somewhat limited resources by the rich and powerful.

Summary

Stealing permeates the Judeo-Christian tradition resulting in serious consequences for mankind. Stealing even threatened the very fabric of the Hebrew community which valued unity, fairness, and equality because everyone depended on very limited yet basic resources. An elementary judicial system based on a notion of God's attributes of justice and mercy in time sought to protect vague notions of property which have further expanded as property rights have expanded in modern times. By New Testament times, theft was often associated with the ambitions of the greedy rich, who still not being content with their sumptuous possessions, often did not consider the material needs of the poor.

---

[178] John Calvin. *Institutes of the Christian Religion*, trans. Ford Lewis Battles, 2 vols., Library of Christian Classics, 20–21 (Philadelphia; Westminster, 1960), II.VIII.45] quoted in Philip Graham Ryken *Written in Stone: The Ten Commandments and Today's Moral Crisis* (Phillipsburg, NJ: P&R Publishing, 2010), 172.

[179] Martin Luther. *The Large Catechism* (Philadelphia: Fortress, 1959), 39 quoted in Philip Graham Ryken *Written in Stone: The Ten Commandments and Today's Moral Crisis* (Phillipsburg, NJ: P&R Publishing, 2010), 172.

How Committed Are Americans to Not Stealing?

Stealing is a broad concept that takes a range of different forms, several of which we will examine in this chapter. The annual Federal Bureau of Investigation (FBI) "Crime Clock Statistics" provide an interesting way to reflect on the prevalence of these types of crimes.

In 2016, there was one larceny theft (taking another's property, except cars, without the threat or use of force) every 5.6 seconds in the United States. Every 20.9 seconds, a home was burglarized; every 41.3 seconds, someone stole a car; and every 1.6 minutes, a robbery occurred (taking another's property with the threat or use of force).[180]

As mentioned in Chapter 6, each year, the FBI collects a tremendous amount of crime data from federal, state, county, local, and university law enforcement agencies across the country. The data is compiled into the Uniform Crime Report (UCR) and is made available to everyone. In total, there were well over eight million larceny thefts, robberies, burglaries, and motor vehicle thefts reported in 2016.

Figure 8.1 indicates the rates of various forms of stealing since 1960. Overall, each type of crime follows a similar trend. There were lower rates of larceny theft (1,035 occurrences per 100,000 people), robbery (60 per 100,000), and motor vehicle theft (183 per 100,000) in 1960 that gave way to a rapid rise into the eighties and nineties and then reversed direction to steadily return to lower levels by 2016. Specifically, the rates per 100,000 inhabitants of larceny theft (over 3100), motor vehicle theft (over 650), and robbery (over 250) topped out in the 1990s while burglary rates hit a maximum in 1980 (1,684). Since these high points, there has been a steady decline in the rates of all four types of stealing—burglary even dropping below the 1960 rate.

---

[180] Federal Bureau of Investigation. 2016. "2016 Crime in the United States." Retrieved November 10, 2017 (https://ucr.fbi.gov/crime-in-the-u.s/2016/crime-in-the-u.s.-2016/resource-pages/figures/crime-clock).

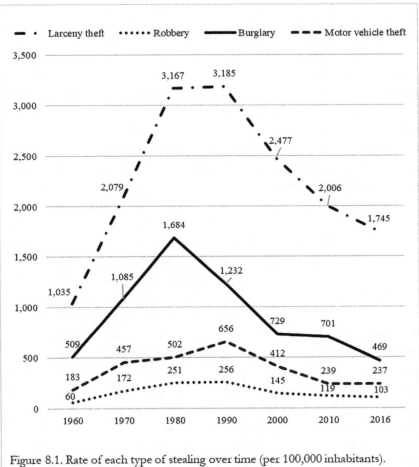

Figure 8.1. Rate of each type of stealing over time (per 100,000 inhabitants). Source: FBI, Uniform Crime Report.

Lest we seem partisan, elitist, or unfair, we thought it wise to take a look at forms of white-collar theft as well. In 2011, the Federal Trade Commission estimated that about 38 million incidents of fraud impacted over 25 million US adults, or about 11% of the adult population. Indeed, there were a combined 7,228 mortgage, health-care, and securities fraud cases investigated by the FBI. Collectively, these cases resulted in $11.4 billion in restitution orders, over $1.2

billion in fines, and 2,212 convictions. Overall, it is estimated that fraud costs $40 to 50 billion annually in the United States.[181]

Identity theft is another form of crime and is on the rise in the United States. In 2012, 16.6 million people sixteen years of age and older were victims of identity theft. This equates to roughly 7% of that population. Combined, these thefts caused victims almost $25 billion in losses. The Bureau of Justice Statistics reported that very few (only about 1 in 10) victims of identity theft report it to the authorities and that this type of crime disproportionately affects people with higher incomes.[182]

When it comes to individual attitudes and beliefs about stealing, there are a few interesting bits of information we can consider. The 2011 World Values Survey consists of data collected from a random sample of 2,232 adults in the United States. Respondents were asked to indicate on a scale of 1 (never justifiable) to 10 (always justifiable) how they felt about various types of dishonesty, some related to stealing. We have presented their responses in Figure 8.2, starting with what the highest percentage of people felt was unjustifiable. By an over 6% margin, the highest percentage of individuals felt they could never justify "stealing property." In total, 76% of respondents were absolutely averse to the behavior. Likewise, the majority of Americans believed "cheating on taxes if you have a chance" (70%), "claiming government benefits to which you are not entitled" (64%), and "avoiding fare on public transport" (53%) could never be considered justified. The highest average on a scale from one to ten was 2.6 indicating that even the people who thought it could be justified typically still leaned heavily toward considering it unjustifiable.

---

[181] US Department of Justice. Office of Justice Programs. The Office for Victims of Crime. Financial Crime. 2016. Retrieved November 10, 2017 (https://docs.google.com/viewer?url=https://ovc.ncjrs.gov/ncvrw2016/content/section-6/PDF/2016NCVRW_6_FinancialCrime-508.pdf).

[182] US Department of Justice. Office of Justice Programs. The Office for Victims of Crime. Financial Crime. 2016. Retrieved November 10, 2017 (https://docs.google.com/viewer?url=https://ovc.ncjrs.gov/ncvrw2016/content/section-6/PDF/2016NCVRW_6_FinancialCrime-508.pdf).

On these attitudinal measures, the age disparities are clear (Figure 8.2). The older people are, the more likely they are to find all the behaviors indefensible. In fact, a minority of eighteen- to twenty-nine-year-olds believe claiming government benefits that one is not entitled to (46%) and avoiding public transportation fares (35%) were never justifiable. About 58% of the youngest group thinks people should never steal for any reason while nearly 90% of the oldest cohort feels it should never occur. A similar but smaller difference is found when it comes to cheating on taxes. Four in ten people under age twenty-nine believe it could be justified while only two out of ten people over sixty feel the same way. This same trend is repeated to varying degrees for all measures.

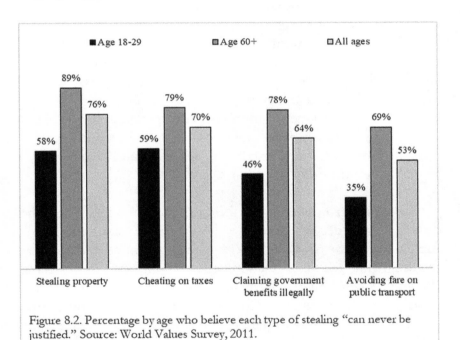

Figure 8.2. Percentage by age who believe each type of stealing "can never be justified." Source: World Values Survey, 2011.

Another interesting way to examine the commandment not to steal is to consider it in the context of an ethical dilemma. The Measuring Morality Study surveyed 1,519 randomly selected adults in the United States and posed a question to measure how individuals deal with such dilemmas.[183] Respondents were asked to consider what a person should do in the following situation:

> In Europe, a woman was near death from a special kind of cancer. There was one drug that doctors thought might save her. It was a form of radium that a druggist in the same town had recently discovered. The drug was expensive to make, but the druggist was charging ten times what the drug cost to make. He paid $200 for the radium and charged $2,000 for a small dose of the drug. The woman's husband, Heinz, went to everyone he knew to borrow the money, but he could only get together about $1,000, which was half of what it cost. He told the druggist that his wife was dying and asked him to sell it cheaper or let him pay later. But the druggist said, "No, I discovered the drug and I'm going to make money from it." So Heinz got desperate and began to think about breaking into the man's store to steal the drug for his wife. Should Heinz steal the drug?

The answer options given included "Yes, he should steal the drug," "I can't decide," and "No, he should not steal the drug." Almost half of the people (49%) responded that he should not steal the drug while the other respondents were split between not being able to decide (23%) and agreeing that stealing is okay in this situation (28%). Interestingly, almost 80% of those who attend church weekly believed stealing would be wrong in this circumstance while half as many who never attend church felt this way. While factors like income and education did not seem to influence how people

---

[183] Vaisey, Stephen. 2012. Measuring Morality Study. The data were downloaded from the Association of Religion Data Archives, www.TheARDA.com, and were collected by Stephen Vaisey.

answered the question, active religiosity seemed to play an important role in shaping people's perceptions about how to make this decision.

When thinking about the generational differences in attitudes, one must wonder if the views of younger people will change with age or if the younger generation will hold to different ways of thinking about these issues until the end of their lives. Only time will tell. Either way, there is no question that there are millions of instances of theft occurring in the United States, but most forms of the crime are not as prevalent as they were thirty years ago. Does this mean we are doing well keeping this commandment? It is up to you to decide, but in the meantime, we turn to exploring honesty more generally.

COMMANDMENT 9

＋━━━◆◆◆━━━＋

"Thou shalt not bear false witness"

Bearing false witness, like stealing, results in disunity, legal troubles, and sometimes even death for the accused. The Hebrew noun *rea* found in this commandment can sometimes be rendered as *neighbor* and can also refer to a "companion, neighbor, friend, fellow citizen." *Rea* always refers to a person with whom one stands in a reciprocal relationship, and in legal contexts, it refers to a fellow member of the covenant community.[184] Although in the Bible, the term *neighbor* (*rea*) can mean someone of any nationality living nearby, as in Exodus 11:2 and Proverbs 3:29 and 27:10, in biblical law, a neighbor is usually a fellow Israelite.[185]

One's reputation in ancient times was paramount. One Proverb teaches that "a good name is to be chosen rather than great riches, and favor is better than silver or gold" (Proverbs 22:1). This commandment may have been derived from a desire to alleviate problems found in Genesis.[186] God, as a lawgiver, attempted to provide social

---

[184] John I. Durham. *Exodus Word Biblical Commentary* (Waco: Word, 1987), 296.

[185] Michael Coogan. *The Ten Commandments: A Short History of An Ancient Text* (New Haven: Yale University Press, 2014), 88.

[186] Alan M. Dershowitz. *The Genesis of Justice: Ten Stories of Biblical Injustice that Led to the Ten Commandments and Modern Law* (New York: Warner Books, 2000), 250–251. Dershowitz noted, "Thou shalt not bear false witness against thy neighbor"—derives directly from Potiphar's wife bearing false witness against Joseph and Joseph then bearing false witness-even as a pretense—against

justice through the law of witnesses. Procedures were eventually for-
mulated in later times about proper forms of witnessing in Hebrew
legal procedure. Leviticus 5:1 states that a witness is anyone who can
testify on the basis of something he has heard or personally seen.

Likewise, Proverbs 29:24 stresses that such a person is morally
obligated to declare what he knows. To attempt to preserve objectiv-
ity, a testimony from at least two people had to be provided before
guilt could reasonably be established (Numbers 35:30; Deuteronomy
17:6, 19:15). When the method of punishment was stoning, the witnesses cast the first stones (17:7)."[187] The court procedure established
the truth without testifying under oath. "False evidence not only hin-
dered the administration of justice in any particular case, but also
undermined public confidence in the integrity of the judicial system—and thereby jeopardized the very stability of society."[188]

In Israelite law, very great significance was attached to the testimony of the witness, seeing that the responsibility for proof lay
with the accused.[189] For this reason, many blessings and harsh consequences were pronounced upon those who were honest or dishonest
about others' actions. In Psalm 15:1–3 (NIV), the question is asked,
"Lord, who may dwell in your sacred tent? Who may live on your
holy mountain? The one whose walk is blameless, who does what

---

his own brothers. Yehuda's [Judah's] desperate question "How can we clear ourselves?" is answered by this prohibition and by the subsequent procedural safeguards that rest on this commandment. Moreover, the earliest biblical narratives
support the right of an accused person to a defense—at least against God. God
gives Adam and Eve an opportunity to defend themselves and gives Cain the
same right. Abraham defends the people of Sodom. God also insists on com-
ing down to earth to see for Himself whether the Sodomites deserve destruction. Hearsay is not good enough even for God. He insists on direct eyewitness
observation. But the clan of Shechem is given no opportunity to defend itself
against human vengeance. Nor are other victims of human injustice. The need
for procedural safeguards against false accusations by human beings is evident."

[187] Dan Lioy. *The Decalogue in the Sermon on the Mount* Studies in Biblical
Literature 66 (New York: Peter Lang, 2004), 78.

[188] Nahum M. Sarna. *The JPS Torah Commentary: Exodus* (New York: JPS, 1991), 114.

[189] J. J. Stamm with M. E. Andrew *the Ten Commandments in Recent Research*
(Naperville, Alec R. Allenson, 1967), 111.

is righteous, who speaks the truth from their heart; whose tongue utters no slander, who does no wrong to a neighbor, and casts no slur on others." The psalmist exclaims to God, "You destroy those who speak lies" (Psalm 5:6). In 1 Kings 21:13 (KJV), it says, "There came in two men, children of Belial, and witnessed against Naboth, saying, Naboth did blaspheme God and the king:' and their witness took away his life." But the Lord warned, "A false witness shall not be unpunished" (Proverbs 19:5 KJV).

Therefore, in the Mosaic Law, "if the witness be a false witness, and has testified falsely against his brother; then shall ye do unto him, as he had thought to have done unto his brother;' if, for instance, he had thought to have taken away his life, his own life shall go for it" (Deuteronomy 19:18–19 KJV). People often have many reasons to lie. "Fear, contempt, revenge, boastful conceit, fraud, and the desire to shine by telling a good story are other motives which prompt lies."[190] Even a truthful statement can be a cruel hurt to a fellow human being. Destructive perversions of the truth can damage life in a tightly bound covenant community.

In ancient Israel, the occasions demanding public truth-telling most frequently were those that regulated public affairs. When disputes occurred, the elders or the judges would call for the disputants to make their presentations and bring along their witnesses.[191] Witnesses formed the basis of law that the Decalogue prescribed to create an environment of justice and mercy. If witnesses became corrupt by knowingly bearing false witness, Israel's divine system of justice became null and void. This commandment became associated with God's justice and even mercy toward the innocent. What people say about others has potential positive and negative consequences for others. Gossip even can legitimate leaders and is an important mechanism of informal social control. However, it can also distract from a God belief and his Law.[192] Perhaps for this reason one reads in the

---

[190] J. I. Packer. *The Ten Commandments* (Wheaton: Tyndale House, 1989), 64.

[191] Walter Harrelson. *The Ten Commandments and Human Rights* (Philadelphia: Fortress, 1980), 143.

[192] Bruce J. Malina and Richard L. Rohrbaugh. *Social-Science Commentary on the Synoptic Gospels* 2nd Edition (Minneapolis: Fortress Press, 2003), 367.

Talmud that "one who bears evil tales almost denies the foundation of faith . . . anyone who bears evil tales will be visited by the plague of leprosy . . . Of him who slanders, the Holy One, blessed be He, says: He and I cannot live together in the world. As it is said: Whoso slanders his neighbor in secret, him will I destroy."[193] According to an old rabbinic saying, slander "kills three: the one who speaks it, the one who listens to it, and the one about whom it is spoken."[194]

By New Testament times, bearing false witness is associated with Satan's temptations of Jesus (Matt. 4). Satan and other evil spirits sometimes tempt Jesus's apostles and even possess the bodies of Israelites. In fact, Satan's very name in the Greek of the New Testament, *diabolos*, means gossiper, backbiter, or slanderer, and was later transliterated into the English word *devil*. Satan was considered a liar and a father of lies (John 8:44). Pride resulted in false witness in court against Jesus (Matthew 26:59) and Stephen (Acts 6:13), which resulted in false convictions, abuse, and cruelty by means of tortuous and demeaning public executions.

Jesus's half-brother, James, discussed the importance of controlling one's language in his epistle. He wrote, "Those who consider themselves religious and yet do not keep a tight rein on their tongues deceive themselves, and their religion is worthless" (James 1:26 NIV). Furthermore "But the tongue can no man tame; it is an unruly evil, full of deadly poison" (James 3:8 NIV). John the Revelator saw in his vision that liars belong "in the lake that burns with fire and sulfur" (Revelation 21:8) and that "everyone who loves and practices falsehood" will be shut out from his eternal city forever (Revelation 22:15).

Some Christians of all historical periods were obsessed with correctly formulating religious doctrine, known as orthodoxy. As a result of defining and redefining orthodoxy, some felt it necessary to

---

[193] (*b. Arakin* 15b). Quoted in Bruce J. Malina and Richard L. Rohrbaugh. *Social-Science Commentary on the Synoptic Gospels* 2nd Edition (Minneapolis: Fortress Press, 2003), 367.

[194] Goran Larsson. *Bound for Freedom: The Book of Exodus in Jewish and Christian Traditions* (Peabody, MA: Hendrickson, 1999), 153 is quoted in Philip Graham Ryken *Written in Stone: The Ten Commandments and Today's Moral Crisis* (Phillipsburg, NJ: P&R Publishing, 2010), 177.

label others with differing theological views as liars and even heretics. These perceived heretics were often cruelly tortured and murdered when, after being questioned by authoritative religious figures of their time and place, they were turned over to the state to be punished by heinous forms of public execution. Bearing false witness during the historical periods of the Inquisition, the Reformation and Counterreformation, made social conditions especially difficult and even deadly for marginalized individuals and groups. Later, in reaction to the excesses of these periods of Christian history, the Puritan Thomas Watson wrote, "He that raises a slander, carries the devil in his tongue; and he that receives it, carries the devil in his ear."[195]

Summary

God always gave individuals a chance in the Hebrew tradition to defend themselves and be witnesses to truth, so this commandment made it possible for this practice to occur among God's covenant people. Largely because of impure motives, ancient Mediterranean peoples, like all human beings, were inclined to speak untruths about others in the most important of matters to get what they wanted, which led to the death of many perceived heretics in early modern Europe. This commandment attempts to remedy the potential detriment to individuals and society at large by prohibiting bearing false witness against a neighbor.

How Committed Are Americans to Not Bearing False Witness?

The measures of dishonest behavior that sociologists tend to track relate to theft, fraud, and other more serious matters that we have already addressed in earlier chapters. Obviously, many of the findings related in the last chapter on stealing reflect a willingness to be dishonest. Consequently, in this chapter, we will focus primarily on what Americans believe about dishonest behavior and even what

---

[195] Thomas Watson. *The Ten Commandments* (1692; repr. Edinburgh: Banner of Truth, 1965), 169–170.

they claim they would and wouldn't do in this regard for a price. There are many interesting and perhaps even unusual measures associated with this commandment, both in terms of what people think is okay and what they actually do.

We start with the 2016 General Social Survey that asked people to indicate their perceptions of the honesty of others in society. Based on the data, it seems that the level of trust Americans have for others has declined over time. Just over half of Americans in 1980 believed they could not trust people, but that number was up to almost 65% of the population in 2016 equating to an almost 25% increase (see Figure 9.1). Likewise, there has been an increase in the number of respondents who think that people will try to take advantage of others, though the change is not as dramatic. About a third of participants in 1980 assumed people would take advantage of others, and that was up to 41% in 2016, a 20% increase.

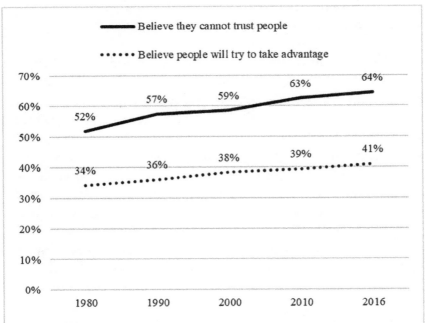

Figure 9.1. Views about the trustworthiness and fairness of others over time. Source: General Social Survey.

The 2012 Measuring Morality Study collected data from 1,519 randomly selected individuals in the United States to explore moral differences in the daily lives of members of the population.[196] Participants were asked several questions that can help us understand their views about and adherence to the ninth commandment. One series of questions begins with the following:

> Many people are used to thinking about morality as it relates to a few controversial public-policy issues: abortion, gay marriage, gun control, the death penalty, etc. This survey is instead about the things people do in their own daily lives. Below you'll be presented with a variety of situations and asked to say whether certain behaviors in those situations would be morally wrong. Please use the following scale from 1 to 7, to indicate the degree to which you judge the behavior to be wrong (if at all).

They were instructed to select 1 if they considered the behavior to be "not at all wrong; has nothing to do with morality" and a 7 to indicate they thought the behavior to be "very wrong; an extremely immoral action". Figure 9.2 shows the percentage of respondents who believed each behavior to be very wrong and extremely immoral. It is evident that only in the case of "faking an injury to collect on insurance" did the majority of respondents feel compelled to take the most extreme moral stance available. In fact, only a quarter of respondents took that stance when it came to "an eighteen-year-old girl breaking an abstinence vow to have premarital sex," while about 40% viewed "lying about a test score when reporting performance to a teacher," and "parking in a handicapped parking spot when not handicapped" as extremely immoral.

---

[196] Vaisey, Stephen. 2012. Measuring Morality Study. The data were downloaded from the Association of Religion Data Archives, www.TheARDA.com, and were collected by Stephen Vaisey.

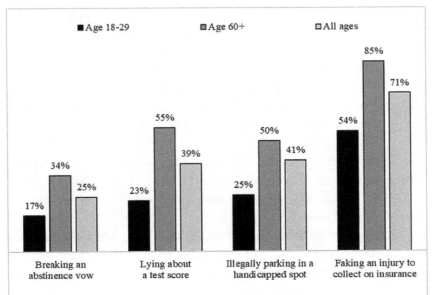

Figure 9.2. Percentage by age who believe each behavior is "very wrong; an extremely immoral action." Source: Measuring Morality Study, 2012.

Again, we find the age differences to be significant and clear. Twice as many of the oldest generation (34%) think it is very wrong to break an abstinence pledge compared to the youngest (17%). Similar ratios are found in relation to lying to a teacher about a test scores. About one in four of eighteen- to twenty-nine-year-olds placed it in the extremely immoral category compared to 55% of the sixty-plus group. Likewise, the differences between the oldest and youngest exist when it comes to illegally parking in a handicap spot (25% vs. 50%) and engaging in insurance fraud (54% vs. 85%). Overall, the mean scores on the 1 to 7 scale suggest that in all cases, Americans collectively lean toward the behaviors being immoral, but it is interesting to note that breaking an abstinence pledge is significantly closer to being considered morally neutral than all the rest of the measures (see Figure 9.2).

Saying things are wrong is one thing, but what if there was money on the line? Would that persuade people to bear false witness? The Measuring Morality Study also asked individuals the following:

> Try to imagine actually doing the following things, and indicate how much money someone would have to pay you, (anonymously and secretly) to be willing to do each thing. For each action, assume that nothing bad would happen to you afterwards. Also assume that you cannot use the money to make up for your action.

Respondents could answer that they would "do it for free" (which was given a score of 1), for $10, $100, $1,000, $10,000, $100,000, $1 million dollars or more, or "never for any amount of money" (scored as an 8).

Again, we will focus on the rate at which people responded no amount of money would convince them to engage in the behavior, thus representing the maximum indication that they believe engaging in the behavior is wrong.

Americans overall lean heavily toward claiming they would never do any of the questionable behaviors. We found a mean unwillingness of 6.7 on a scale of 1 to 8 to "cheat in a game of cards played for money with some people you don't know well," and averages of over 7, on that same scale, in regard to saying "something bad about your nation (which you don't believe to be true) while calling in, anonymously, to a talk-radio show in a foreign nation," signing "a secret-but-binding pledge to only hire people of your race in your company," or throwing "out a box of ballots during an election to help your favored candidate win."

About 40% of those surveyed claimed they have a price when it comes to cheating in a card game, 32% would lie about their country anonymously to a foreign talk show for money, but only about 20% would throw away election ballots or pledge to only hire individuals of their own race for a price. In all these cases, people who say they have a price tend to claim their price is very high (see Figure 9.3).

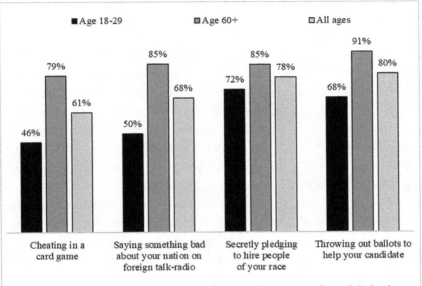

Figure 9.3. Percentage by age who claim they would not engage in each behavior for "any amount of money." Source: Measuring Morality Study, 2012.

The price at which the younger people can be bought to engage in these actions is considerably lower in every situation. As has been the general pattern throughout the book, the oldest and youngest cohorts find themselves at the extremes with numbers rising or falling incrementally as age increases. A slight majority of eighteen- to twenty-nine-year-olds say they would cheat in a card game or say something untrue about their nation on a foreign talk show for money, while significantly fewer adults over sixty would do the same in either case (21% and 15% respectively). Likewise, nine out of ten in the over sixty age group could not be convinced to throw out a box of ballots to help their candidate win while many fewer under age 29 (68%) claim to be that resistant to the idea. Interestingly, when it comes to signing a secret pledge to hire members of the same race, the gap between the age groups is less substantial. About 72% of the youngest would never do it while 85% of the oldest group would always refuse.

Taking one more measure from the 2011 World Values Survey, we find that 76% of respondents indicated it is never justifiable to take a bribe, and as has been the pattern, older people are considerably more likely to say it is always wrong than younger people are. In fact, only 58% of individuals under the age of thirty believed the action to be unjustifiable compared to almost 87% of those over the age of fifty.[197]

To explore how well teenagers are keeping the ninth commandment, we examined more data from the 2003 National Study of Youth and Religion. Teens were asked how often they lied to their parents in the last year and how often they cheated on schoolwork. Perhaps unsurprisingly, the majority of teenagers did both. Eighty-four percent said they lied, but only about 10% said they did it often. Significantly fewer youth reported cheating in school (62%), with only 7% doing it often. Of those who actually confessed to either of these acts, about half reported engaging in the behaviors only rarely.

We will end on a different note, but a very relevant one. It is interesting to observe that the legal system sees relatively few slander or libel cases, which might be considered the most literal interpretation of this commandment.

In a 2005 survey of jurisdictions in the United States, out of 26,948 civil bench and jury trials, only 175 involved accusations of slander or libel, and in only 39% of those cases was the plaintiff declared the winner. Such cases represented fewer than 1% of all civil court trials.[198]

A Pew Research Center report found that 67% of Christians believe "being honest at all times" is "essential to what being Christian means to them," but that leaves a significant percentage who do not view it as core to Christianity.[199] Evidently, there are Americans who seem willing to do dishonest things for a price and who hesitate to claim specific dishonest behaviors are extremely immoral.

---

[197] World Values Survey Wave 6 2010–2014. Official Aggregate v. 20150418. World Values Survey Association (www.worldvaluessurvey.org). Aggregate File Producer: Asep/JDS, Madrid, Spain.

[198] Langton, Lynn, and Thomas H. Cohen. 2009. "Civil Bench and Jury Trials in State Courts, 2005". U.S. Department of Justice. Retrieved December 2, 2017 (https://www.bjs.gov/index.cfm?ty=pbdetail&iid=369)

[199] Pew Research Center. 2016. "Religion in Everday Life." Retrieved December 19, 2017 (http://www.pewforum.org/2016/04/12/religion-in-everyday-life/).

Are there enough who do so that we can argue the United States is effectively keeping the ninth commandment? It is definitely something to think about as we shift our focus to matters of desire and the commandment not to covet.

COMMANDMENT 10

"Thou shalt not covet"

The commandment to not covet assisted one to keep the other nine. Covetousness eroded gratitude, which was central to God's covenant relationship with his people. The other nine commandments could be observed merely by means of an external or formal action. This final commandment prohibited the inner instinct that led to breaking other commandments.[200] In addition, greed became the root of many perceived problems in ancient Israel.

Although God had given commandments to Abraham so that "he may command his children and his household after him that they may keep the way of the Lord, to do righteousness and justice" (Genesis 18:19), these generalities had failed to produce an end to lawlessness, deception, and even murder. More specific rules, with prescribed sanctions, were necessary."[201] Jacob, later called Israel, renewed the Abraham covenant and resisted covetousness when he exclaimed, "I have enough" (Genesis 33:11). The later Mosaic Law not to covet provided even more sanctions about what it was appropriate and inappropriate to desire.

---

[200] Walter C. Kaiser, Jr. *The Expositor's Bible CommentaryExodus* (Grand Rapids: Zondervan, 1990), 425–426.

[201] Alan M. Dershowitz. *The Genesis of Justice: Ten Stories of Biblical Injustice that Led to the Ten Commandments and Modern Law* (New York: Warner Books, 2000), 251.

Nuances in the Hebrew language define what it means to covet. The term "to covet" (*hamad*) in this commandment can mean "desire," "covet," or "lust after," and only sometimes does it express both the desire for something and the making of plans to secure the desired object.[202] In addition, in very old Phoenician inscriptions containing the verb *hamad* it was used to describe the ambitions of a foreign king, chief, or ruler to put himself into possession of a newly built city. One such inscription reads, "Or if he [that is, the foreign king] covets this city and tears down this door . . ."[203] Coveting is associated with conquering cities and their inhabitants in the Near East. In Deuteronomy, the wife is named first as a person one covets. "Neither shalt thou desire thy neighbour's wife, neither shalt thou covet thy neighbour's house" (Deuteronomy 5:21 KJV).

Many passages from the Old Testament refer to a wide spectrum of sin, crime, and error that are consequences of coveting. The prophet Micah admonished Israel for not following the tenth commandment:

> Woe to those who plan iniquity, to those who plot evil on their beds! At morning's light they carry it out because it is in their power to do it. They covet fields and seize them, and houses, and take them. They defraud people of their homes, they rob them of their inheritance. (Micah 2:1–2 NIV)

In a more specific narrative in 1 Kings 21, Ahab wanted Naboth's vineyard, which resulted in Naboth's murder and the confiscation of his property. To covet was to be like the daughter of the horse-leech who exclaimed, "Give, give" (Proverbs 30:15) because she felt entitled. Those who coveted were never satisfied and could even draw up

---

[202] Walter Harrelson. *The Ten Commandments and Human Rights* (Philadelphia: Fortress, 1980), 148–149.

[203] J. J. Stamm with M. E. Andrew. *The Ten Comm andments in Recent Research Studies in Biblical Theology* Second Series 2 (Naperville: Alec R. Allenson, Inc., 1967), 103.

the Jordan River into their mouths (Job 40:23) and were despised by the Lord (Psalm 10:3).

Later in Colossians 3:5, Paul explains that coveting is actually idolatry because these coveted things become your god, and then unfortunately they will control your life. Achan (Joshua 7:21) and Judas (John 12:6) acted for money's sake, and it led to their death (Matthew 26:14–16, 48–50 and 27:3–5). Paul warned Timothy of covetousness (1 Timothy 6:10 KJV) as the root of all evil because coveting money "led to snares and other foolish lusts." We read in 2 Peter that because of covetousness, false "teachers will exploit you with fabricated stories" (2 Peter 2:3 NIV). The Dead Sea Scrolls also warn that the movers of sedition are motivated by covetousness (1QpHab 8.11–13).[204] In Matthew 6:25–34, worry is the cousin of covetousness that leads the disciples to not be faithful to their master (God) and instead to serve the master named Mammon (extreme amounts of wealth). Philo also explained that covetousness leads to estrangement of kinsmen, hatred, and even war "that bring disaster to the human race."[205]

Jesus cautioned his disciples to not be preoccupied with plans to accumulate material possessions. He best expressed these teachings in the "Parable of the Rich Fool" (Luke 12:13–21 NIV):

> Someone in the crowd said to him, "Teacher, tell my brother to divide the inheritance with me." Jesus replied, "Man, who appointed me a judge or an arbiter between you?" Then he said to them, "Watch out! Be on your guard against all kinds of greed; life does not consist in an abundance of possessions." And he told them this parable: "The ground of a certain rich man yielded an abundant harvest. He thought to himself, 'What shall I do?

---

[204] Bo Reicke. *The Epistles of James, Peter and Jude* The Anchor Bible (New York: Doubleday, 1964), 162.

[205] Philo. *Decalogue* 151–153; Solomon Goldman *The Ten Commandments* (Chicago: University of Chicago Press, 1956), 187.

I have no place to store my crops.' Then he said, 'This is what I'll do. I will tear down my barns and build bigger ones, and there I will store my surplus grain. And I'll say to myself, "You have plenty of grain laid up for many years. Take life easy; eat, drink and be merry."' But God said to him, 'You fool! This very night your life will be demanded from you. Then who will get what you have prepared for yourself?' This is how it will be with whoever stores up things for themselves but is not rich toward God."

Jesus taught his followers that instead of harboring covetous desires to having even more material possessions by means of securing an inheritance or enlarging one's agricultural surplus, they should focus on laying up treasures in heaven (Matthew 6:20). This involved becoming a committed disciple as outlined in the Sermon on the Mount (Matthew 5:7), and giving up improper desires, possessions, and actions. Jesus listed coveting along with the heinous crimes of theft, murder, and adultery (Mark 7:21–22).

Another means to avoid coveting was to be content with one's current situation, which prevented other problems and negative consequences. According to Paul, contentment discourages individuals from coveting others' things. Paul said, "I have coveted no man's gold or silver" (Acts 20:23 KJV). Paul wrote, "I have learned, in whatsoever state I am, therewith to be content" (Philippians 4:11 KJV). Paul truly did choose to be happy although he experienced persecution, physical hardships, and other misfortunes (2 Corinthians 11) as he evangelized. Paul summarized his thoughts on this commandment when he wrote, "Since, then, you have been raised with Christ, set your hearts on things above, where Christ is seated at the right hand of God. Set your minds on things above, not on earthly things" (Colossians 3:1–2).[206]

---

[206] For a discussion on this subject, see Edmund P. Clowney *How Jesus Transformed the Ten Commandments* (Phillipsburg, NJ: P&R Publishing, 2007), 146.

James pointed out that "what causes quarrels is that we fight because we covet and cannot obtain, so you fight and quarrel" (James 4:1–2). The apostle Paul warned that people who covet will not inherit the kingdom of God (1 Corinthians 6:9–10). Centuries later, Augustine wrote, "The law said, 'Thou shalt not covet,' in order that, when we find ourselves lying in this diseased state, we might seek the medicine of grace."[207]According to Augustine, without this mystical grace as defined by neo-Platonic philosophy, sins were commonly committed because the sinner had some particular good in mind that he wished to enjoy as the result of his sin. For example, a man killed another because he coveted his wife or his goods (*Confessions* II, iv, 9).[208] Many other later Christian thinkers including Bede, Anselm, Aquinas, Luther, Calvin, and Barth have argued that the human will was corrupted or at least weakened because of the Adam's Original Sin, so coveting is inevitable.[209]

Therefore according to this somewhat deterministic and arguably orthodox view, some individuals had been predestined by God's grace to be saved, and therefore their will had become enabled to avoid the sin of coveting. Also, according to this view, because of the utterly depraved nature of mankind, the non-elect must be doomed to unwisely covet the things of others.

Summary

Coveting, derived from innermost personal selfish desires instead of being filled with gratitude, potentially leads to transgressing many of the other nine commandments. Greed has often led to disregarding God and has resulted in the crimes of murder, adultery, lying, theft, and the sin of bearing false witness against one's neigh-

---

[207] Augustine. *On Original Sin* 32 in Philip Schaff *Nicene and Post-Nicene Fathers* Vol. 5; St. Augustin: Anti-Pelagian Writings (New York: The Christian Literature Company, 1887), 276. Also quoted in Mark F. Rooker *The Ten Commandments: Ethics for the 21st Century* (Nashville: B&H, 2010), 172.

[208] Gerald Bonner. *St. Augustine of Hippo: Life and Controversies* (Norwich: Canterbury Press, 1986), 54.

[209] See Brent J. Schmidt. *Relational Faith* (forthcoming).

bor. If one could avoid the universal sin of greed, certainly other commandments would be easier to keep.

How Committed Are Americans to Not Coveting?

It would be perfectly acceptable for us to claim that the commandment not to covet has already been well covered in the other chapters. Someone who steals is clearly coveting material possessions or the money to be made from them. When someone commits adultery, they are acting on a desire to have another person's husband or wife. Indeed, much of the dishonesty that occurs in society is the result of people trying to obtain something that they assume honesty will not provide.

Measures we have used in other chapters regarding what people are willing to do for money could all easily be presented here as indicators of coveting. But of course, we want to make sure a book about the Ten Commandments has an individual chapter for each, so we have more to present that we hope will pique each reader's interest.

When it comes to directly measuring people's inner desires and motivations as they might relate to coveting, the data is sparse. Consequently, in this chapter we will use measures that would be considered less direct indicators of what we are trying to understand, and we do not claim that all of what you will see here is ideal for the task at hand. We do believe, however, that it all reflects the essence of what coveting is—self-centered desire or wanting things which one does not have, including wanting more of what one already has.

At the heart of the commandment not to covet is the idea of being happy with what one already has. Dissatisfaction with circumstances might be a sign of craving something more for oneself. The General Social Survey provides us with a few interesting measures to consider that allow us to track trends over time.

Respondents were asked, "Taken all together, how would you say things are these days? Would you say that you are very happy, pretty happy, or not too happy?" Figure 10.1 reveals the percentage who responded they were not too happy. While there certainly are some fluctuations, they are not too extreme, though the slightly lower percentage of unhappy people in 1990 and 2000 is interesting. More recently, the number seems to be hitting a high point, 14% of Americans reporting being unhappy in 2016.

Participants were also asked, "So far as you and your family are concerned, would you say that you are pretty well satisfied with your present financial situation, more or less satisfied or not satisfied at all?" Most years, about twice as many people are unhappy about their financial situations as they are with life in general. The rate tends to be fairly consistent at around 26–27% over the last several decades, though there are highs and lows that extend another few percentage points on either side of that.

Likewise, since 1990, 11–14% of Americans report experiencing at least some dissatisfaction with the work they do when asked, "On the whole, how satisfied are you with the work you do? Would you say you are very satisfied, moderately satisfied, a little dissatisfied or very dissatisfied?" Overall, the vast majority of Americans seem to be satisfied in all these areas of life (see Figure 10.1).

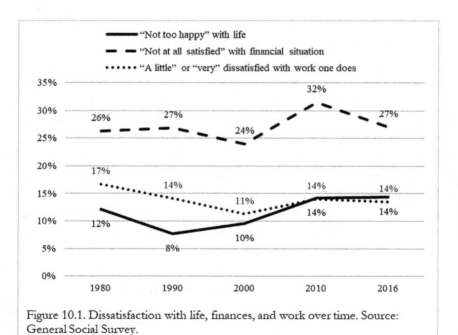

Figure 10.1. Dissatisfaction with life, finances, and work over time. Source: General Social Survey.

Perhaps a more direct measure we can examine relates to home ownership. The Census Bureau recorded that the average size of single-family houses in the United States has steadily increased from 1,660 square feet in 1973 to 2,640 in 2016.[210] This represents an almost 60% increase in size. Even so, a survey of 2,000 Americans conducted by Harris Poll for the real estate website Trulia in 2017 revealed that only 32% of respondents would choose to live in a house that has the same size as their current house, while 37% want a bigger house and 23% would prefer a smaller house if they moved in the next year.[211] Ultimately, the majority of respondents want a different sized house. Since the study was not based on probability sampling, we cannot generalize to the United States population, but the results do give us some idea of the extent to which people might want houses they do not have.

Since coveting is in its essence wanting more than one has, it stands to reason that debt could be another indicator of it. If people are spending money they do not have to get more of what they want, it could be considered a sign of covetous desires. Unfortunately, the data provide us no direct way to filter debt used for material needs vs. debt used for wants, so the reader must be cautious when interpreting this data.

In 2011, the Census Bureau reported the average household debt in America, including households with no debt, as $126,809. Of the 41% of households with debt on a home, the average mortgage amount was $151,315 while the average debt on a vehicle was $13,288, with about a third of Americans in vehicle debt.

Examining unsecured debts, we find just under 40% of households had credit card debt, the average amount being $7,697. About 7% of households had other loans averaging $28,483 and about 19% of households averaged $26,541 in other debt. Overall, 69% of households held some sort of debt in 2011, with almost 40%

---

[210] United States Census Bureau. Retrieved December 9, 2017 (https://www.census.gov/construction/chars/pdf/squarefeet.pdf).

[211] McLaughlin, Ralph. 2017. "Americans (Can't Get No) Home Size Satisfaction." Retrieved on December 9, 2017 (https://www.trulia.com/blog/trends/home-size-survey-march-16/).

of them in debt over $50,000, including 10% with a total of over $250,000 in debts.[212]

As mentioned earlier, while there are many questions in many surveys asking Americans what they want, very few questions directly ask what they want for themselves. For example, researchers often ask how people feel about the government redistributing wealth, but not if they want it redistributed to themselves. Still, we did find a few interesting questions that get at what people desire and may be considered, at least indirectly, related to coveting.

During the 2012 Measuring Morality Study, adults in the United States were presented a series of statements and asked, "How much does each of the following statements sound like you?" They could respond "very much like me" (scored as a 1), "like me," "sometimes like me," "a little like me," "not like me," or "not like me at all"(which received a score of 6).We have isolated those who reported each statement was very much like or like me and indicated responses in Figure 10.2. All of these statements indicate a desire to get something that is wanted and thus can be related to the tenth commandment.[213]

---

[212] United States Census Bureau. 2011. "Debt by Year." Retrieved December 19, 2017 (www2.census.gov%2Fprograms-surveys%2Fdemo%2Ftables%2F-wealth%2F2011%2Fwealth-asset-ownership%2Fdebt-tables-2011.xlsx).

[213] Vaisey, Stephen. 2012. Measuring Morality Study. The data were downloaded from the Association of Religion Data Archives, www.TheARDA.com, and were collected by Stephen Vaisey.

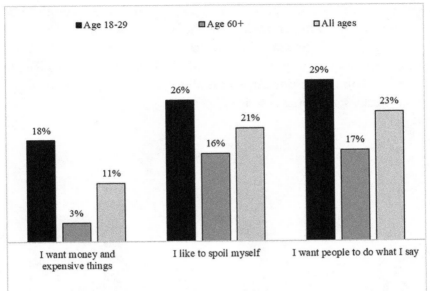

Figure 10.2. Percentage by age who reported each statement is "very much like me" or "like me." Source: Measuring Morality Study, 2012.

One of the measures we might get the least push-back about in this chapter is whether people agree with the statement "It is important to me to be rich. I want to have a lot of money and expensive things." As Figure 10.2 shows, only a small percentage of individuals (10%) view themselves this way, though eighteen- to twenty-nine-year-olds are six times more likely than people over sixty to think the statement is like them (18% vs. 3%). Similar trends are found for the other statements. In all cases, younger people are considerably more likely to think of themselves the way the statements suggest. In total, 21% of those surveyed claimed to agree with the statement, "Having a good time is important to me. I like to 'spoil' myself," and 23% felt "It is important to me to get respect from others. I want people to do what I say."

In Figure 10.3, we see an even higher percentage, 27%, who felt they could describe themselves with the statement, "It's very important to me to show my abilities. I want people to admire what I do," while a similar percentage (28%) found the phrase, "Being very successful is important to me. I hope people will recognize my achievements," to match their persona. "I seek every chance I can to have fun. It is important to me to do things that give me pleasure" was accepted as a characteristic by almost 35% of US adults. In all cases, the younger respondents were about 1.5 to 2 times more likely to think the statements described them.

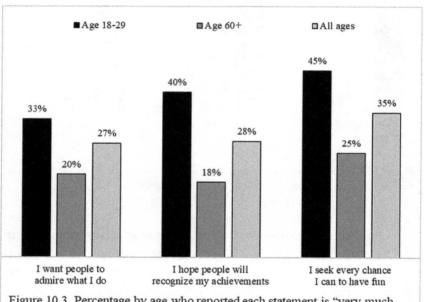

Figure 10.3. Percentage by age who reported each statement is "very much like me" or "like me." Source: Measuring Morality Study, 2012.

When asked if they love to shop, about a third of Americans agreed that they do. In total, 32% of people over sixty love it while an even greater number of the youngest generation agree (39%). The only one of the statements presented in any of these figures that the average person agrees with or thinks describes them is "I just don't have enough money to live the life I would like to live." Two-thirds of Americans agreed with the statement, and the mean reveals an overall tendency to agree as well. Of course, as anyone reading at this point should expect, significantly more of the under thirty cohort (66%)

agree with the statement compared to the 53% of the oldest generation, but all age groups lean toward agreement (see Figure 10.4).

It must be noted that ultimately, a strong majority of Americans do not believe any of these statements describe them well except the last one about not having enough money to live the life they want. Indeed, the average scores for all the other statements indicate a general disregard for these characteristics among the American population. There are, nonetheless, many people who seem to accept these characteristics as their own. Does that mean America is struggling with the tenth commandment? As always, we leave that up to you to decide.

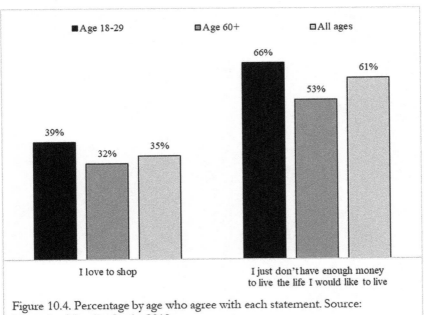

Figure 10.4. Percentage by age who agree with each statement. Source: Measuring Morality Study, 2012.

CONCLUSION

W e now know what you are thinking. How can a book like this
have a chapter called "Conclusion" when no real arguments
were made and the authors came to no definitive conclusions about
how committed the United States is to the morality promoted by the
Ten Commandments?

In corresponding about finalizing this work, one of the authors
emailed the other asking whether we should create this chapter and
the response was, "I could try to write a conclusion, but I am wor-
ried that it will come across as very biased. Usually conclusions sum-
marize the main points, but I'm not sure we really have a point to
conclude." Upon receiving this reply, the other author laughed out
loud, knowing that this statement was true about this work's lack of a
thesis. It is certainly a unique organizing principle to allow the reader
to come to his or her own conclusions about public morality.

Our goal has been to present information and evidence related
to America's commitment to the Ten Commandments and then to
allow you, the reader, to completely formulate conclusions about
what it all ultimately means. If you are also unsure about what to
conclude from the discussion of each commandment and its modern US application and need something practical to take away from
it—something useful to now understand—you could think about
what you may have learned about human nature based on the inter-
pretative history and data you have curiously perused. Perhaps we all
can agree that human nature is unpredictable, surprising, and not
completely good or bad.

Of course, as authors, we have our own biases about this topic
and our own ideas about what it means to be a moral society. We
certainly could have quite easily presented our own assertive and

dogmatic analyses of each piece of data we found. Despite this, and as difficult as it was for us, we really tried to refrain from doing so. Why? Because we want every reader to ponder these issues on their own, unfettered by our subjective viewpoints. We want you to think, to consider, to feel, to worry, to celebrate, to hope, to judge, to wish, and to come to understand what you really think about the moral state of the United States of America.

Certainly, we would be hesitant to claim that we perfectly achieved our ideal. We understand that some might consider the very detailed measures of each commandment that we used as a sign of bias, though we tried to use the best measures we could find, given our understanding of the commandments in the context of their common historical and modern interpretations. Unfortunately, sometimes, we simply could not find ideal measures, so we did the best we could with what data was available.

We hope that anyone with concerns regarding our choices who can point us in a better direction will let us know what better data could have been utilized for potential future editions. Despite a lack of perfection in our data selection, we strongly believe what we have presented in the preceding chapters can be helpful for all who are interested in pondering questions related to American morality and ethics. If nothing else, this is a starting point to consider how people self-report their actions on moral questions. All are now invited to delve deeper into what each data source has to say about what people in the United States feel, think, and sometimes even do.

We are also aware that some individuals might not care as much about whether or not Americans are keeping the Ten Commandments. We assume that if you didn't care at all about the answer to this question, you would not have purchased and read this book, let alone made it as far as this conclusion. One early reviewer of a proposal for this work went so far as to claim we were asking the wrong question and argued that it would be better to ask whether Americans even want to keep the Ten Commandments. It is certainly worth considering what type of morality Americans want or what might be desirable and even ideal, and the analysis presented here could provide insights into what the answer to that question might be. Still, we hope our readers will go beyond that.

We hope each reader, when pondering what we have presented here, will consider what greater or lesser commitment to morality, as outlined by the Ten Commandments, might mean for themselves, their families, their communities, and the United States as a whole. For example, there are clear and often stark differences in attitudes and behaviors between Bible believers and non-believers and between Jews and Christians and the religiously non-affiliated. Is one group living in a way that results in what should be considered better adjusted individuals, stronger families, or a stronger nation? Is the dramatic rise in the percentage of individuals choosing not to affiliate with organized religion a sign of joyful liberation from long-held and foolish traditions, or does it reflect the loss of something that brings truth, common purpose, and needed solidarity for society to function? Are the extensive household resources Americans pour into entertainment and recreation a sign of reaching the goal of having more fulfilling lives, or should we be concerned with the lack of time and money Americans put toward their more transcendent or otherworldly pursuits? Can a society reach its potential when older people do not get enough respect? Can individuals and families thrive when a significant proportion of people believe it is okay to break pledges and lie to teachers and agree that engaging in insurance fraud can sometimes be justified? Do a lack of satisfaction and a desire to be recognized or have more expensive things drive people to new heights that bring about the best of what humans can do, or do they result in jealousy and bitterness toward others who have more? Are the disparities between the younger and older generations a cause for celebration or a cause for alarm? These and many other questions can be pondered further in light of the information presented in this book. We hope you continue to contemplate them and we have provided data that may be helpful in doing so.

Obviously, from a biblical perspective, engaging in behaviors associated with the "Thou shalt nots" results in negative outcomes, and doing activities promoted by the "Thou shalts" promotes the welfare of all. From this perspective, adherence to the Decalogue is essential to the stability and success of individuals, families, and society. To others, however, adhering to some of these principles, at least in the ways commonly accepted by religious believers, can result in unhappiness and has potentially damaging effects on society. Would we be better or worse off as a result of improved adherence to the Ten Commandants as measured in this book? We will leave that for you to decide.

What does it mean to be moral? Am I moral? Should I be moral? Can we even know what morality is? How should we decide what is moral? All around us, there are strong opinions about what should and should not happen in society, including what individuals should or should not do or think. Most Americans are sympathetic to at least some of the teachings of the Decalogue and some regularly use it as a yardstick of morality. Based on perceptions of public morality, political and social interest groups often accuse the opposition of destructive and even evil motives. Those on the extremes of each side seem to want to silence their opposition, sometimes on the basis of morality. We hope that what we have presented will also help to motivate individuals to examine further what people really think and believe about moral questions before they make assumptions and attack them.

Moreover, it would benefit all readers to be kinder and more sympathetic to others after learning about how they perceive right and wrong, good and evil, and answers to specific controversial and moral questions. We hope each reader discovered something surprising or unexpected in this book. Perhaps similar discoveries will occur as each of us leave our comfort zones to consider the viewpoints and behaviors of those whose ideas, beliefs, and behaviors may be construed as different and even antithetical to our own.

As noted throughout this book, we refuse to tell you what to think, but we feel very comfortable pleading with you to give the issue of morality in America more thought. We encourage all to consider the implications of what some in our society promote as a moral life. Do the values endorsed by the Decalogue enhance society or propel it toward decline? Is the fact that the younger generation is thinking about morality differently from the older generation a good thing or a bad thing? Are there elements of the Decalogue that should be encouraged more? Are there some that should be discouraged? What would they be and how do we know? How should we decide which values, beliefs, and behaviors to endorse society-wide? What does a society look like when it adheres to all the Ten Commandments, and what would it look like if it opposed them all?

We have provided a snapshot of some current trends and trends over time that we hope will fuel this worthwhile discussion, but it falls upon each of us to make these decisions for ourselves after careful pondering. In the end, we just sincerely desire that all readers will become better, kinder, and more thoughtful individuals through contemplating these moral questions.

REFERENCES

Afroprofile. *Value of the entertainment and media market in the United States from 2011 to 2020 (in billion U.S. dollars)*. https://www.statista.com/statistics/237769/value-of-the-us-entertainment-and-media-market/ (accessed February 26, 2018).

Arnold, John H. *Belief and Unbelief in Medieval Europe* (NY: Hodder Arnold, 2005),

Bates, Matthew. *Salvation by Allegiance Alone* (Grand Rapids: Baker, 2017)

Bonner, Gerald. *St. Augustine of Hippo: Life and Controversies* (Norwich: Canterbury Press, 1986)

Braaten, Carl E. and Seitz, Christopher R. eds. *I am the Lord Your God: Christian Reflections on the Ten Commandments* (Grand Rapids: Eerdmans, 2008)

Brown, Peter. *The Rise of Western Christendom* (Oxford: Blackwell, 1997)

Bureau of Labor Statistics. 2017. "American Time Use Survey User's Guide". Retrieved January 27, 2018 (https://www.bls.gov/tus/atususersguide.pdf).

Bureau of Labor Statistics. 2017. "Unpaid Eldercare in the United States—2015–16 Summary." Retrieved December 19, 2017 (https://www.bls.gov/news.release/elcare.nr0.htm).

Calvin, John *Institutes of the Christian Religion*, trans. Ford Lewis Battles, 2 vols., Library of Christian Classics, 20–21 (Philadelphia; Westminster, 1960)

Cannon, William Ragsdale. *History of Christianity in the Middle Ages* (Nashville: Abingdon, 1960)

Carmichael, Calum M. *The Ten Commandments* (Oxford: The Ninth Sacks Lecture, 1983)

CBS News. 2012. "Q&A: Why Kids Kill Parents." Retrieved December 22, 2017 (https://www.cbsnews.com/news/qa-why-kids-kill-parents/)

Centers for Disease Control and Prevention. "Abortion Surveillance Report." Retrieved November 11, 2017 (https://www.cdc.gov/reproductivehealth/data_stats/abortion.htm).

Charles, R. H. *The Decalogue* (Eugene, OR: Wif and Stock, 2004)

Chrysostom, John. *On Wealth and Poverty*, trans. Catherine Roth (New York: St. Vladmir's Seminary, 1984)

Clowney, Edmund P. *How Jesus Transformed the Ten Commandments* (Phillipsburg, NJ: P&R Publishing, 2007)

Coogan, Michael. *The Ten Commandments: A Short History of An Ancient Text* (New Haven: Yale University Press, 2014)

Daniell, David. *William Tyndale: A Biography* (New Haven: Yale University Press, 1994)

Death Penalty Information Center. 2017. "Facts about the Death Penalty." Retrieved November 11, 2017 (https://docs.google.com/viewer?url=https://deathpenaltyinfo.org/documents/FactSheet.pdf)

Dershowitz, Alan M. *The Genesis of Justice: Ten Stories of Biblical Injustice that Led to the Ten Commandments and Modern Law* (New York: Warner Books, 2000)

Dunnam, Maxie D. *Exodus,* The Communicator's Commentary (Waco, TX: Word, 1987)

Durham, John I. *Exodus Word Biblical Commentary* (Waco: Word, 1987)

Federal Bureau of Investigation. 2016. "2016 Crime in the United States." Retrieved November 10, 2017 (https://ucr.fbi.gov/crime-in-the-u.s/2016/crime-in-the-u.s.-2016/resource-pages/figures/crime-clock)

Ginzberg, Louis. *The Legends of the Jews* (Baltimore: John Hopkins University Press, 1998)

Giving USA 2017: The Annual Report on Philanthropy for the Year 2016, a publication of Giving USA Foundation, 2017, researched and written by the Indiana University Lilly Family School of Philanthropy. Available online at www.givingusa.org.

Goldman, Solomon. *The Ten Commandments* (Chicago: University of Chicago Press, 1956)

Harrelson, Walter. *The Ten Commandments and Human Rights* (Philadelphia: Fortress, 1980)

Henry Chadwick *The Church in Ancient Society: From Galilee to Gregory the Great* (Oxford: Oxford University Press, 2003)

Herodotus *Histories* translated by David Grene (Chicago: University of Chicago Press, 1988)

Horton, Michael S. *The Law of Perfect Freedom* (Chicago: Moody, 2004)

Kaiser, Walter C. Jr. *The Expositor's Bible Commentary Exodus* (Grand Rapids: Zondervan, 1990)

Kloppenborg, John S. and Wilson, Stephen G. eds. *Voluntary Associations in the Greco-Roman World* (New York: Routledge, 1996)

Langton, Lynn, and Thomas H. Cohen. 2009. "Civil Bench and Jury Trials in State Courts, 2005". U.S. Department of Justice. Retrieved December 2, 2017 (https://www.bjs.gov/index.cfm?ty=pbdetail&iid=369)

Larsson, Goran. *Bound for Freedom: The Book of Exodus in Jewish and Christian Traditions* (Peabody, MA: Hendrickson, 1999),

Lioy, Dan. *The Decalogue in the Sermon on the Mount* Studies in Biblical Literature 66 (New York: Peter Lang, 2004)

Luther, Martin. *The Large Catechism,* trans. Robert H. Fischer (Philadelphia: Fortress, 1959)

MacCulloch, Diarmaid. *The Reformation* (New York: Penguin, 2005)

Malina, Bruce J. and Rohrbaugh, Richard L. Social-Science Commentary on the Synoptic Gospels 2nd Edition (Minneapolis: Fortress Press, 2003)

Masci, David. 2017. "5 Facts about the Death Penalty." Pew Research Center.

McLaughlin, Ralph. 2017. "Americans (Can't Get No) Home Size Satisfaction." Retrieved December 9, 2017 (https://www.trulia.com/blog/trends/home-size-survey-march-16/)

Monson, Quin and Scott Riding. 2016. *Sabbath Day Observance in the U.S.* Retrieved December 19, 2017 (https://www.deseretnews.com/media/misc/pdf/DNN-Ten-Today-Sabbath.pdf)

National Baptist Convention. 2017. "About Us." Retrieved December 15, 2017 (http://www.nationalbaptist.com/about-us/index.html)

Nielsen, Eduard. *The Ten Commandments in New Perspective* (London: SCM Press, 1968)

Packer, J. I. *The Ten Commandments* (Wheaton: Tyndale House, 1989)

Parker, Kim and Juliana Menasce Horowitz. 2015. "Family Support in Graying Societies." Pew Research Center. Retrieved December 15, 2017 (http://www.pewsocialtrends.org/2015/05/21/family-support-in-graying-societies/)

Parker, Kim and Juliana Menasce Horowitz. 2015. "Family Support in Graying Societies." Pew Research Center. Retrieved December 15, 2017 (http://www.pewsocialtrends.org/2015/05/21/family-support-in-graying-societies/)

Pelian, Jaroslav and Hotchkiss, Valerie. eds. *Creeds and Confessions of Faith in the Christian Tradition Volume: Early, Eastern, & Medieval* (New Haven: Yale University Press, 2003)

Pew Research Center. 2010. "U.S. Religious Knowledge Survey." Retrieved November 15, 2017 (http://www.pewforum.org/2010/09/28/u-s-religious-knowledge-survey).

Pew Research Center. 2013. "A Portrait of Jewish Americans." Retrieved December 19, 2017 (http://www.pewforum.org/2013/10/01/chapter-4-religious-beliefs-and-practices/)

Pew Research Center. 2016. "Religion in Everyday Life." Retrieved December 19, 2017 (http://www.pewforum.org/2016/04/12/religion-in-everyday-life/).

Philo. *On the Decalogue, On the Special Laws, On the Virtues* in the Loeb Classical Library, 320, ed. E. H. Warmington, trans. F. H. Colson (Cambridge: Harvard University, 1998)

Propp, H. C. *Exodus 19-40 The Anchor Bible* (New York: Doubleday, 2006)

Ratzinger, Joseph Aloisius (Pope Benedict XVI) *Great Christian Thinkers* (Minneapolis: Fortress, 2011)

Reicke, Bo. *The Epistles of James, Peter and Jude* The Anchor Bible (New York: Doubleday, 1964

Rooker, Mark F. *The Ten Commandments: Ethics for the 21ˢᵗ Century* (Nashville: B&H, 2010)

Ryken, Philip Graham. *Written in Stone: The Ten Commandments and Today's Moral Crisis* (Phillipsburg, NJ: P&R Publishing, 2010)

Sarna, Nahum M. *The JPS Torah Commentary: Exodus* (New York: JPS, 1991)

Southern Baptist Convention. 2017. "Fast Facts about the Southern Baptist Convention." Retrieved December 15, 2017 (http://www.sbc.net/fastfacts/)

Stamm, J. J. with Andrew, M. E. *The Ten Commandments in Recent Research Studies in Biblical Theology* Second Series 2 (Naperville: Alec R. Allenson, Inc., 1967)

The Church of Jesus Christ of Latter-day Saints. 2017. "Facts and Statistics." Retrieved December 14, 2017 (https://www.mormonnewsroom.org/facts-and-statistics/country/united-states)

The People of the United Methodist Church. 2017. "United Methodists At-A-Glance." Retrieved December 15, 2017 (http://www.umc.org/news-and-media/united-methodists-at-a-glance)

Thiessen, Gerd. *A Theory of Primitive Christian Religion* trans. John Bowden (London: SCM Press, 1999)

Twitter Counter. 2017. "Twitter Top 100 Most Followers." Retrieved December 14, 2017 (https://twittercounter.com/pages/100)

Twitter. 2017. Retrieved December 14, 2017 (https://twitter.com/?lang=en)

United States Bureau of Labor Statistics. *2016 Consumer Expenditure Survey.* Retrieved December 19, 2017 (https://www.bls.gov/cex/)

United States Census Bureau. 2011. "Debt by Year." Retrieved December 19, 2017 (www2.census.gov%2Fprograms-surveys%2Fdemo%2Ftables%2Fwealth%2F2011%2F-wealth-asset-ownership%2Fdebt-tables-2011.xlsx).

United States Census Bureau. 2016. "Square Feet of Floor Area in New Single-Family Houses Completed." Retrieved December 9, 2017 (https://www.census.gov/construction/chars/pdf/squarefeet.pdf)

United States Department of Justice. Office of Justice Programs. The Office for Victims of Crime. "Financial Crime 2016." Retrieved November 10, 2017 (https://docs.google.com/viewer?url=https://ovc.ncjrs.gov/ncvrw2016/content/section-6/PDF/2016NCVRW_6_FinancialCrime-508.pdf)

Veyne, Paul *When Our World Become Christian: 312-394* Translated by Janet Lloyd (Cambridge: Polity, 2010).

Watson, Thomas. *The Ten Commandments.* Grand Rapids, MI: Christian Classics Ethereal Library (First published as a part of A Body of Practical Divinity, 1692)

Whitford, David M. *A Reformation Life: The European Reformation through the Eyes of Philipp of Hesse* (Santa Barbara: Praeger, 2015)

Wilcox, Michael. *Fire in the Bones: William Tyndale Martyr* (Salt Lake City: Deseret, 2014)

DATASETS

Baylor University. 2005. *The Baylor Religion Survey, Wave I.* Waco, TX: Baylor Institute for Studies of Religion [producer].

Baylor University. 2010. *The Baylor Religion Survey, Wave III.* Waco, TX: Baylor Institute for Studies of Religion [producer].

Putman, Robert D., and David E. Campbell. 2011. *Faith Matters Survey.* The Association of Religion Data Archives [distributor]. http://www.thearda.com/Archive/Files/Descriptions/FTHMAT11.asp.

Smith, Tom W, Peter Marsden, Michael Hout, and Jibum Kim. General Social Surveys, 1972–2016 [machine-readable data file] /Principal Investigator, Tom W. Smith; Co-Principal Investigator, Peter V. Marsden; Co-Principal Investigator, Michael Hout; Sponsored by National Science Foundation. -NORC ed.- Chicago: NORC at the University of Chicago [producer and distributor].

The National Study of Youth and Religion, http://youthandreligion.nd.edu/, whose data were used by permission here, was generously funded by Lilly Endowment Inc., under the direction of Christian Smith, of the Department of Sociology at the University of Notre Dame and Lisa Pearce, of the Department of Sociology at the University of North Carolina at Chapel Hill.

Vaisey, Stephen. 2012. Measuring Morality Study. The data were downloaded from the Association of Religion Data Archives, www.TheARDA.com, and were collected by Stephen Vaisey.

World Values Survey Association. 2014. World Values Survey Wave 6 2010-2014 OFFICIAL AGGREGATE v.20150418. (www.worldvaluessurvey.org). Aggregate File Producer: Asep/JDS, Madrid SPAIN.

INDEX

Page numbers in **bold** indicate figures

Jewish 2, 8, 10, 12, 22, **23**, **24**, 28, 31, 42, **49**, **50**, 54, 55, 60, 89
Jews 4, 12, 20, 24, 44, 45, 48, 53, 60, 139
Job 7, 18, 89, 126
John 18, 54, 65, 66, 76, 90, 115, 126
Joseph of Egypt 7
Joshua 102, 126
Judah 53
Judaism 4, 6, 7, 45, 49, 65
Judas 76, 126
Judeo-Christian tradition 4-6, 20-23, 25, 28-30, 43, 44, 55, 67, 105
Judges 16
Judith 54

killing 4, 7-10, 45, 67, 76-79, **80**, 81, 82, 85, 89, 116, 127, 128
1 Kings 5, 17, 28, 114
2 Kings 16
kinship (see: family)

Latter-day Saints (Mormons) **24**, 33
leisure 34, **35**, **36**, 53
lesbianism (see: sexuality)
Leviticus 4, 8, 53, 64, 66, 88, 102
love 4, 9, 10, 18, 25

Luke 29, 54, 55, 65, 76, 91, 103, 126
Luther, Martin 11, 19, 78, 92, 105, 128
Lutherans 12, **24**
lying (see: false witness, lying)

Malachi 88
manslaughter (see: killing)
marriage 5, 7, 88-95, 97, **98**, 118
satisfaction **98**, 131, 139
Matthew 4, 9, 29, 42, 54, 66, 76, 77, 90, 103, 115, 126, 127
media 31, 39, 93
Methodists **24**, 33
money, spending and attitudes 18, 37-39, 47-49, 60, 67, 68, 105, 110, 119-121, 126, 129, 131, **133**, 134, 135, 139
Mormons (see: Latter-day Saints)
mortgage (see: debt)
Mosaic Law 2, 4, 10, 66, 67, 93, 102, 103, 114
Moses 2-5, 11, 16, 17, 19, 64, 66, 93
motor vehicle theft (see: stealing, motor vehicle theft)
murder (see: killing)

Naboth 114

ABOUT THE AUTHORS

Michael K. Abel earned a PhD in sociology from the University of Washington. He specializes in the study of religion and has published research on a variety of topics including religious retention and faith. Dr. Abel is interested in questions related to morality, religiosity, and religious conviction. He and his wife, Patricia, are parents of six children.

Brent J. Schmidt earned a PhD in classics from the University of Colorado-Boulder. He specializes in Greek and Latin moralistic texts and has published (or will soon publish) works on biblical word studies and the New Testament. Dr. Schmidt enjoys teaching and studying ancient languages and culture. He and his wife, Judith, are parents of one son.

CPSIA information can be obtained
at www.ICGtesting.com
Printed in the USA
FSHW02n0159300718
50937FS